Childlike Faith
for
Grown-Up Miracles

The Journey of a Baby Christian

Chantale Williams

Edited by Christina M. Frey

Acknowledgments

First and foremost, all the glory and honor goes to God.

Secondly, to my amazing husband, Elton—you were instrumental in God's plan for my rescue. Your tenacious pursuit of His ways was just the example I needed to bring me to the right place at the right time while doing the right thing in faith. Thanks for loving me, encouraging me, and believing in me when I doubted my purpose. Your confidence in me pushed me to thrive when quitting seemed like the better option. I can't thank you enough for your unwavering support. I love you!

To my babies—you'll always be my babies, Vivianna and Elton Jr. I love you more than words can express. Your very presence in my life means God trusts me with His precious children. Thanks for all the mommy time you sacrificed so I could write this book. Thanks for encouraging me by picking up your own pens and imitating me writing. I cherish the words of wisdom both of you have imparted without realizing it. Because of you, I know it's never too late or too early to follow my dreams.

To my coworker, Suzanne Taylor—the day you told me that God spoils baby Christians, you changed how I viewed God. I no longer saw Him as a distant, inaccessible being but rather as a real person who wanted me to be happy. Thanks to you, I know Him as Daddy. Thanks for listening to the stories of my first encounters with God and for igniting the flame to write this book. You probably had no idea how profoundly that one statement would change the course of my life. God used you, honey!

To all my pastors who labored in the Word and taught me how to seek God for myself, thank you! To every conference guest speaker who confirmed the Word for me with personal stories, thanks for paving the way. To all my family and friends who supported me along my journey, and who could've stopped believing in me or even stopped listening when procrastination got the best of me, thank you! Yes, Brigette Kirk, I'm mostly referring to you here. Love ya!

To my longtime friend, Sharon—thanks for telling me about that book. One person plants the seed, and another waters it, but God brings the increase. You've done a lot of watering over the years. Thank you!

Thanks, Narline, for keeping me calm and making sure I didn't act out of character!

Thanks, Donetta Quinones, for the valuable insight you provided during our consultations. You helped me work through a difficult chapter, and I'm better for it.

Keiko Anderson, I learned the most profound lesson on relationships through you. When I think of you, Hebrews 6:12 comes to mind: "Don't drag your feet. Be like those who stay the course with committed faith and then get everything promised to them" (MSG). Love your style, love your grace—you set the pace.

About This Book

Dear Reader and Friend,

When I rededicated my life to God in January 2007, I was fascinated by how God began constantly revealing Himself to me through His miraculous power. As I shared some of my testimonies with a coworker, she made this profound statement: "God spoils baby Christians."

Immediately I envisioned a newborn baby and a loving parent. I imagined the parent doing everything for the baby, like diaper changing and bottle feeding, trying to establish trust and make a connection with their child. I wondered if babies really do milk it, or whether parents just enjoy spoiling them.

My daughter was less than a year old at the time, and I likened God's love for me to my love for her: unconditional. I reasoned that if God really does spoil baby Christians, then I would not miss out on this part of my journey—I was going to milk it through great expectation. And just like a doting parent establishing a relationship and fostering dependence, God held my hand and began walking me through this way of life.

The more I got to know Him, the more He became my master orchestrator. I am still amazed by His attention to detail and the way He weaves the lives of others into mine with such impeccable timing and harmony.

My journey as a baby Christian, I realize, has been a journey of childlike faith. With every baby step I took in faith, God performed a very grown-up miracle, and it seemed like there was never a good stopping point to end this phase. That is, of course, until now.

It's come to an end, not because He's obsolete or His powers have faded in my life, but because when I was a child I spoke, thought, and reasoned like a child, and now I'm, well, grown...

I know Him for myself. I know His love never fails me—though others may. I know that I overcome by the blood of the Lamb and the words of my testimony (Rev. 12:11). My stories serve as contemporary reminders that God doesn't change. He's still the same today as He was yesterday and will be forever.

What He did for me, He can do for you.

This book is where I share my stories and the fundamental truths that were in operation even when I didn't know it. I hope you will appreciate my transparency. Take advantage of the Childlike Faith Exercises and seal your actions with the Prayers included at the end of each chapter. All Scripture quotations, unless otherwise indicated, are taken from the King James Version of the Holy Bible. Sometimes I'll mix in other translations to drive a point home; I love The Message and Amplified versions of the Bible and will use these much of the time. You may also find it useful to access Bible Gateway (http://www.biblegateway.com) whenever I share Scripture.

Now get ready to enjoy my labor of love, be saturated in faith, and experience unprecedented miracles in your own life.

In faith,

Chantale

Childlike Faith for Grown-Up Miracles

Table of Contents

Chapter 1

Radically Rescued

Imagine this: You just experienced a head-on collision with an eighteen-wheeler that spun you into several other cars before coming to a screeching halt. You're spiraling out of control, certain this will end in death, but somehow you walk away from the scene unscathed. Though shaken, you're overwhelmed with gratitude because your life was spared, and you vow to make the most of every precious moment thereafter. That's exactly how I felt when I had my epiphany.

Rededicating my life to God filled me with a deep sense of joy and undeniable hope that allowed me to see Jesus in the smallest details of my life. I was a whole new person, filled with God-given purpose and always on the lookout for opportunities to be used for His glory. I was so satisfied that it was difficult to picture how and why I'd ever lost sight of God's blessings that were trying to chase me down. I kept looking in the rearview mirror of my life, but my memory didn't always serve me well; try as I might, I couldn't pinpoint the freeway or the exit where I'd ditched the promise of the picturesque journey God had created for me.

When did my navigation system reroute me to a dead-end road so far from my destination? How had I lost sight of the principles in God's Word that were meant to guide and protect me? All I knew was that pain had begun dictating my detours, and out of desperation I'd picked up hitchhikers who wanted more than a ride—they wanted to destroy me through insecurity, self-loathing, worry, and fear.

But God was a prayer away and patiently waited for me to turn to Him so He could draw me near. There comes a point when brokenness cries out for the only one who can save it. That happened for me the day I found my husband's cell phone tucked away in a hidden compartment in his truck just a few weeks after he'd left for a yearlong deployment. The voicemail notification showed several unheard messages, and my curiosity got the better of me. What I discovered was devastating. She said she would miss him. She couldn't wait for him to get back so they could spend time together. Finally, proof. I played the message over and over again. My heart was bleeding, and it cried out to heaven in agony. *Help. Courage. Please.*

I was disappointed in him, and he could tell. Even though he was deployed I often answered his phone calls with excuses to end the conversation, if I bothered to answer at all. It didn't matter how long he'd waited in line to call me. I was working on putting emotional distance between us as well.

My daughter was a few months old, and since he'd just left for his deployment, I figured I had almost a year to practice being a single mom. My greatest fear was single parenthood—I had watched my mom struggle with five kids after she and my dad separated and eventually divorced—and besides the financial responsibility, I knew raising kids alone wouldn't be as easy as a Sunday afternoon walk. Yet I was considering it because I was tired of feeling like I wasn't enough for him.

Less than two months after I'd found the

voicemail, he called me and said he'd gotten saved. I'll never forget that day. I thought he'd been saved from a bomb, because the spiritual connotation of the word *saved* didn't register. As much as I despised him it hit me then that he could die over there; after all, he was in Iraq, and I knew of the danger of IEDs detonating. But when I finally understood what my husband was saying, I cursed him and told him I didn't want anything to do with a Bible-toting bleep-bleep.

I hadn't been to church in over a decade. He began to explain, and the more he talked the more fear gripped me. All I could remember were the never-ending rules and rituals: no pants, no makeup, no jewelry, no short skirts, no secular music, no TV, no meat, no working on the Sabbath … The list went on and on. At that time I viewed Christianity as borderline cultish, with congregations of fanatics I should avoid. I believed in God but shunned organized religion.

To my surprise, he didn't really argue with me like he would have in the past. "I'm going to pray that the Holy Spirit touches your heart like He touched mine," he said.

"You do that, then!" I felt like I'd won that argument, because he finally shut up—but I was discounting the power of the Holy Spirit.

During the days after our conversation, I weighed the choices before me. I could continue to deal with Elton and his trifling ways or embrace the new, religious Elton. Even though I'd wanted my husband to change, my sporadic prayers had been shallow. All I'd wanted was for him to spend more time with me, to come home right after the club instead of hours later, and to take me with him and introduce me to all his friends—especially the females. I look back now and realize that some prayers seemed to have gone unanswered because my requests simply weren't God's best for me. My expectations were so low that God couldn't even give me what I wanted.

I wish I could say that I had this Damascus Road experience like Paul or that an angel spoke to me to tell me I would carry the Son of God, like Mary, but it didn't happen that way. I wasn't even sure the decision I was making would work. But although my resolve was weak and my hope faint, it was enough for God to work a miracle in my life. He wanted me to soar and knew that I would need strength, courage, and willpower to shake off those things that weighed me down and prevented me from spreading my wings. When I put my hope in the Lord, He renewed my strength and empowered me to take steps to solidify my position in Him.

I decided that if I was going to do this God thing, I'd better give it a serious try. A few days after my husband's big reveal, I woke up at the break of dawn and dismantled our corner bar by myself. I didn't know then where the supernatural strength and coordination came from, or how I managed to balance the connecting top all the way down my wobbly ladder. I simply knew that I wanted a fresh start. I poured out the alcoholic beverages as a gesture of surrender to God—a surrender of every alcohol-impaired decision I'd ever made, of every time I'd given a piece of myself to the wrong homies who never intended to make a home with me. Pouring the alcohol down the drain released me from them.

Then I went through my closet and got rid of all the porn. I couldn't believe I was holding on to those old VHS tapes even though I had graduated to Internet sites. I surrendered those times when curiosity got the best of me and led me down the path of insatiable lust that distorted my sex life. Watching porn together didn't make it okay. I wanted to give my marriage a fighting chance—to renew the passion between us with only God at the center of it all.

I even threw out my secular music and movies. It was like cleaning out the pantry before going on a diet. The influential lyrics and intoxicating scenes that formed pop culture were the only voices I'd listened to for a very long time. They had shaped my values and seemed more real to me than the Bible stories I'd read as a child and the hymns I'd sung or played on the piano. I didn't know the workings that had trapped me in this lifestyle, but I knew I needed some serious deprogramming.

I was desperate, and God met me where I was and took the little I gave Him and worked it out for my good. That was about nine years ago, and I know now that being in a relationship with God makes every other relationship better.

God can use the least likely person to share His message of love, hope, and salvation. He can use you to plant the seed; He can use me to water the seed; and in the end God brings the increase of souls in the most significant way. When I ponder how God brought me back home, I'm impressed with His choice to use my husband. To me it was God's way of confirming that our love was meant to be in spite of the hard times we'd experienced. It was proof that all things work together in a fitting plan for the good of those who love God and are called according to His design and purpose (Rom. 8:28). I am so blessed; I didn't even love God, but His design and purpose were enough for the restoration to begin.

Although I had long forgiven myself for my past, a nagging voice stopped me from following through with sharing my story. It bothered me that I didn't know when I was blinded to the principles in God's Word or why I'd done some of the things I wanted to share. I felt compassion for the old Chantale, but I wanted to know exactly when and where the downward spiral began.

I looked for logical explanations for my actions, but could find none. I had sinned; there would be no good reasons. I tried to move on, but the unanswered questions were still tucked away in the recesses of my mind.

At the end of February 2015, I attended a women's conference in England. It was my first time in the United Kingdom, but I wasn't there for the sightseeing; I had come with an expectation that God would speak to me.

The conference host started by describing the worst question to ask someone who's lost something. It never fails, she said, that someone will ask, "Where did you lose it?" Of course the response could only be "If I knew where I lost it, it wouldn't be lost, right?" I was overwhelmed by the futility of that question, but in the same breath I hoped that God would give me my answer during the message.

The conference host went on to say that the Holy Spirit knows exactly where we lost it—where we lost our way. I was washed over with relief. Here I was, trying to make sense of how, where, and why I'd lost it, and God was telling me not to worry my pretty head with those details. It didn't matter where and when it had happened; by His power He would restore double and throw some icing on the cake. Thank You, Jesus! I didn't need to remember the places, times, or events. As I journeyed with God, He would orchestrate divine learning opportunities to facilitate restoration (Joel 2:25–26).

Though we can never really understand the

magnitude of God's goodness toward us, every day of gratitude fills us with just a little more insight on how much Jesus loved us when He died for us and completed the work of the cross. As I write this I'm taken back to the garden of Eden. Adam and Eve had everything—provision, purpose, passion, prayer, and paths—and they lost it all, but God still had a plan of restoration.

In the garden, God made to grow every tree that is pleasant to the sight or to be desired, and good or suitable for food; the tree of life was at the garden center, and so was the tree of the knowledge of good and evil (provision) (Gen. 2:9). God gave Adam and Eve dominion over everything and placed them in Eden to tend, guard, and keep it (purpose). They were one—united in one flesh, naked, and unashamed (passion). But most importantly, they were in constant communication with God (prayer).

They also had choice (paths): God gave them authority over everything, but told them that in order to avoid death, they should not touch the tree of knowledge of good and evil.

Adam and Eve were tempted, second-guessed God's word, and ate of the tree. Though they didn't physically die on the spot, death was introduced. They knew what they had done. Immediately they recognized that they werc naked, and they were ashamed enough to sew together fig leaves to cover what we now consider to be private parts. They avoided communication with God by hiding. When God confronted them, the story of what happened came out with lots of finger pointing.

God outlined the consequences of their actions. To the serpent, whom Satan possessed to tempt Eve, He said,

> "Because you've done this, you're cursed,
> cursed beyond all cattle and wild animals,
> Cursed to slink on your belly
> and eat dirt all your life.
> I'm declaring war between you and the Woman,
> between your offspring and hers.
> He'll wound your head,
> you'll wound his heel."

He told the Woman:

> "I'll multiply your pains in childbirth;
> you'll give birth to your babies in pain.

You'll want to please your husband,
but he'll lord it over you."

He told the Man:

"Because you listened to your wife
and ate from the tree
That I commanded you not to eat from,
'Don't eat from this tree,'
The very ground is cursed because of you;
getting food from the ground
Will be as painful as having babies is for your
wife;
you'll be working in pain all your life long.
The ground will sprout thorns and weeds,
you'll get your food the hard way,
Planting and tilling and harvesting,
sweating in the fields from dawn to dusk,
Until you return to that ground yourself, dead
and buried;
you started out as dirt, you'll end up dirt"
(Gen. 3:14–19 MSG).

So God put them out of the garden of Eden,

where they had provision, purpose, passion, and prayer, and left them with the path they'd chosen. But God so loved Adam and Eve—and the world born of them—that He gave His Son "so that no one need be destroyed; by believing in him, anyone can have a whole and lasting life" (John 3:16 MSG).

The curse that God imposed in Genesis 3:16–19 can be reversed by the blessing He gave in John 3:16. To this day, there are paths before us—life and death, blessings and curses—and God asks us to choose life, so that we and our children might live (Deut. 30:19). Satan, our enemy, comes to steal, kill, and destroy, just as he did in the garden of Eden with Adam and Eve. But Jesus came, died, and rose again so that we could have eternal life, and so that our reality might be better than we could ever imagine (John 10:10).

It doesn't matter what our past looks like. Accepting Jesus Christ as our Lord and Savior makes all things new. Anyone who believes in Him "is acquitted; anyone who refuses to trust him has long since been under the death sentence ... [because] of [their] failure to believe in the one-of-a-kind Son of God when introduced to him" (John 3:16–18 MSG).

The problem we face is that God-light, Jesus,

"streamed into the world, but men and women everywhere ran for the darkness ... because they were not really interested in pleasing God. Everyone who makes a practice of doing evil, addicted to denial and illusion, hates God-light and won't come near it, fearing a painful exposure. But anyone working and living in truth and reality welcomes God-light so their work can be seen for the God-work it is" (John 3:19–21 MSG).

When I read that Scripture, the first thing that came to mind was a cockroach. Evildoers are like cockroaches, running from the light because they don't want to be exposed. God's children, though they don't always act quite like it, eventually welcome the light into their hearts even when it exposes them, their wrongdoings, and their flaws; they welcome the light because they trust the process as God's way of preventing and removing the evil in their hearts. This renews their sense of purpose, ignites their passion for God, restores communication through prayer, and makes way for a flow of provision.

The story of the woman at the well illustrates it best (unless otherwise noted, all dialogue and Scriptural quotations in this story are from The

Message translation of John 4:1–30). Jesus was passing through Samaria and decided to rest by a well while the disciples left to buy food for lunch. When a Samaritan woman came by to draw water, Jesus asked her for a drink. She was taken aback; Jews in those days wouldn't be caught dead talking to Samaritans, probably much less a Samaritan woman. But Jesus said, "If you knew the generosity of God and who I am, you would be asking *me* for a drink, and I would give you fresh, living water."

So the woman mocked Jesus, saying, and I paraphrase, "How you gon' try givin' me living water when you don't have a pot to piss in—pardon, you don't have a bucket to draw water with? Who do you think you are? Shooooot, my daddy's daddy's daddy passed this well down to us!"

Jesus said, "Everyone who drinks this water will get thirsty again and again. People who drink the water I give will never thirst—not ever. The water I give will be an artesian spring within, gushing fountains of endless life." It's as if Jesus was telling her she could keep her generational curse if she wanted to, but given the choice, she should choose life—choose what He had to give.

I don't know if the Samaritan woman believed Him at this point, but I think she was being flirtingly sarcastic when she said, "Sir"—with all due respect but not meaning it at all—"give me this water so I won't ever get thirsty, won't ever have to come back to this well again!" I imagine that being thirsty could have a sexual connotation, and she was pushing boundaries because that's the kind of woman she was.

Jesus, in His infinite wisdom, led the conversation right to where He needed her to be for a light exposure. "Go call your husband and then come back."

Like a cockroach, she first attempted to hide. "I have no husband."

Jesus replied, "That's nicely put: 'I have no husband.' You've had five husbands, and the man you're living with now isn't even your husband. You spoke the truth there, sure enough."

Tradition is what she was used to, so she replied, "Oh, so you're a prophet! Well, tell me this: Our ancestors worshiped God at this mountain, but you Jews insist that Jerusalem is the only place for worship, right?" She wasn't acknowledging what God exposed; instead she wanted to get into a religious debate to discredit what was taking place in her life at that very moment.

Jesus reeled her back in. "Believe me, woman, the time is coming when you Samaritans will worship the Father neither here at this mountain nor there in Jerusalem. … God's way of salvation is made available through the Jews. But the time is coming—it has, in fact, come—when what you're called will not matter and where you go to worship will not matter. It's who you are and the way you live that count before God. Your worship must engage your spirit in the pursuit of truth. That's the kind of people the Father is out looking for: those who are simply and honestly *themselves* before him in their worship."

In spite of what Jesus shared, the woman wasn't convinced, but she had a faint hope in the Lord. Although she wasn't sure of the future, she acknowledged that the Messiah was coming and that when He arrived she'd get the whole story.

That's when Jesus revealed Himself to her. "I am he … You don't have to wait any longer or look any further."

When the disciples came back, they were shocked that Jesus was talking to that kind of woman. They didn't say anything, but their faces showed it. The woman took the hint and left hurriedly, leaving her water pot behind, but the impact Jesus had on her was revelatory. In fact, she invited the people in her village to come and see a man who knew all about what she'd done—a man who exposed her and knew her inside and out. She alluded to the fact that He could be the Messiah, and they went out to see for themselves.

I love the fact that Jesus crossed gender and race lines and pursued the woman until her exposure to the light could transform her. In the end, she didn't run off like a cockroach but left with renewed purpose to share the gospel of Jesus Christ. She had been radically rescued.

This is what God wants to do for us. He wants to rescue us from the grip of death in every area of our lives. Jesus wants to give us living water, the continual flow of everything He's intended us to have since the garden of Eden. Then He wants us to share that knowledge and to encourage others to experience Him for themselves. In the garden we were told to be fruitful and to multiply (Gen. 1:28). We can do this not only by bearing natural children, but also by seeing others nurtured in the kingdom of God through the seeds we plant when we share the gospel of Jesus Christ.

Typically we get help from people we trust. That's why it's so important for all people to know that God is the most trustworthy person to seek in their time of need (Rom. 10:14–17). Jesus commissioned us to teach those we encounter in God's way of life and to baptize them in the name of the Father, Son, and Holy Spirit (Matt. 28:19–20).

God knows my story, and through the collective efforts of willing and obedient people who shared His truth, He shed light on the dark areas of my life and transformed me. In the next few chapters I share what God exposed to the light, and the revelations I gained in childlike faith. I pray that it will stir your faith to trust God in the process of your own transformation.

Childlike Faith Exercises

If you haven't accepted Jesus Christ as your Lord and Savior, now's the perfect time. God promises to pour out His Spirit on every kind of person, saints and sinners alike—whoever calls for help will be saved (Acts 2:21). "The word that saves is right here, as near as the tongue in your mouth, as close as the heart in your chest. It's the word of faith that welcomes God ... Say the welcoming word to God— 'Jesus is my Master'—embracing, body and soul, God's work of doing in us what he did in raising Jesus from the dead. That's it. You're not 'doing' anything; you're simply calling out to God, trusting him to do it for you. That's salvation. With your whole being you embrace God setting things right, and then you say it, right out loud: "God has set everything right between him and me!" (Rom. 10:4–10 MSG).

If you've already accepted Jesus Christ into your life, help someone else make the same choice. Be like the woman at the well; run and tell others what God did for you, so that they too may experience the salvation freely given (John 4:28).

Prayer

Read Psalm 139 (MSG) out loud and in the name of Jesus.

God, investigate my life;
get all the facts firsthand.
I'm an open book to you;
even from a distance, you know what I'm
thinking.
You know when I leave and when I get back;
I'm never out of your sight.
You know everything I'm going to say
before I start the first sentence.
I look behind me and you're there,
then up ahead and you're there, too—
your reassuring presence, coming and going.
This is too much, too wonderful—
I can't take it all in!

Is there anyplace I can go to avoid your Spirit?
to be out of your sight?
If I climb to the sky, you're there!
If I go underground, you're there!
If I flew on morning's wings
to the far western horizon,
You'd find me in a minute—
you're already there waiting!
Then I said to myself, "Oh, he even sees me in

the dark!
At night I'm immersed in the light!"
It's a fact: darkness isn't dark to you;
night and day, darkness and light, they're all the
same to you.

Oh yes, you shaped me first inside, then out;
you formed me in my mother's womb.
I thank you, High God—you're breathtaking!
Body and soul, I am marvelously made!
I worship in adoration—what a creation!
You know me inside and out,
you know every bone in my body;
You know exactly how I was made, bit by bit,
how I was sculpted from nothing into
something.
Like an open book, you watched me grow from
conception to birth;
all the stages of my life were spread out before
you,
The days of my life all prepared
before I'd even lived one day.

Your thoughts—how rare, how beautiful!

God, I'll never comprehend them!
I couldn't even begin to count them—
any more than I could count the sand of the
sea.
Oh, let me rise in the morning and live always
with you!
And please, God, do away with wickedness for
good!
And you murderers—out of here!—
all the men and women who belittle you, God,
infatuated with cheap god-imitations.
See how I hate those who hate you, God,
see how I loathe all this godless arrogance;
I hate it with pure, unadulterated hatred.
Your enemies are my enemies!

Investigate my life, O God,
find out everything about me;
Cross-examine and test me,
get a clear picture of what I'm about;
See for yourself whether I've done anything
wrong—
then guide me on the road to eternal life.

In Jesus' name I pray. Amen.

Chapter 2

Forgiven and Forgiving

Radical rescue not only includes being forgiven and made whole from the pain we've inflicted on ourselves, but also taking the sting out of the hurt inflicted by others and replacing it with unmistakable joy and freedom. God is faithful in His promise to get us where we need to be to live out our full potential. Once God dealt with my heart to prevent me from sabotaging my own future, He proceeded with care to ensure that I could forgive those who'd hurt me too.

When I was maybe nineteen or twenty, I was raped. Some may wonder how I could not remember—and for years I too had preconceived notions about how a rape victim would react to these circumstances. Should I even be called a victim? Was it my fault? Did this change me forever?

I didn't realize how much rape had changed me until I attended a women's conference in 2012.

Before the conference began, I had read the speaker's biography and knew of her date rape incident, but I was so desensitized that I quickly skimmed past it. I had a front-row seat but sure wasn't expecting to be a basket case on the topic so many years later. I was more interested in what she could bring to the table as a successful business owner.

On the last day of the conference, the speaker shared the heart-wrenching story of her rape by someone she trusted. She recounted in great detail her journey to recovery, including committing herself to a psychiatric ward to facilitate her breakthrough.

My situation was different, I thought. Initially I had wanted to have sex and had enjoyed the foreplay that preceded the rape. However, when I asked the guy to put on a condom, he only pretended to get one. I asked him again to find one, and he went to his car and pretended once more. Again I realized he didn't have one on.

My value set at the time only had me afraid of catching a sexually transmitted disease or getting pregnant. I told him I couldn't have sex with him— maybe next time. What happened next was a blur. I remember how the look on his face became distorted, and the way he violently pushed me back to the bed and forcibly raped me. When he was done he simply went to sleep.

I was in shock, but I gathered my clothes and walked out the door into the night. It was maybe two o'clock in the morning. I was living in Belize at the time, and there were no buses running, no taxis at that hour, and no open corner stores, and the streets were empty. I walked to the nearest bus stop and sat there until the first bus came by at six o'clock in the morning.

I had no cell phone and no one to call anyway. My parents had recently separated; my mother was back in the United States, and I had moved out of my dad's place within a few weeks of having my first real job. Sitting alone, I analyzed what had happened and took the blame. I was the one who'd thought I was mature enough to be on my own. I was the one who was naked, who didn't have my own condoms. I was the one who'd teased him. I had asked for this.

My parents had warned me about men who only wanted sex; I was the one who hadn't listened. I wasn't even a virgin, so what did it matter? He didn't take anything. There was nothing there. I had simply lost control of a situation I had created. I didn't tell anyone for years, and when I did it was to qualify me to minimize someone else's pain from rape or abuse.

Unlike the guest speaker, though, I didn't hide my shame under baggy clothes; I led a promiscuous life. I brushed over what had happened and resumed control over my sex life. I carried my own condoms, and everyone knew I had them. But when the speaker said that rape wasn't about sex but control, it clicked. I couldn't stop the tears from flowing.

During her psychiatric ward experience she'd had to carry actual sandbags representing the blame she'd taken for what had happened to her. Part of the exercise forced her to carry these sandbags until she was ready to release the blame. As she spoke about the experience, I began to evaluate my own life to see what I was carrying. It was not pretty. What saddened me the most was that I couldn't even let God love me or bless me how He wanted to.

Although I knew His ways were higher than mine, subconsciously I couldn't relinquish control to Him. Unfortunately I'd spent years reliving the event in my mind over and over to the point of depression. I knew I shouldn't dwell on negativity, but I kept getting sucked into the scene and would wallow in hurt. I was so ashamed. I didn't feel like I had the same rights as women who were raped by total strangers. Deep down I knew rape was rape, but I was afraid that people would consider me a tease and deserving of what I got. Being promiscuous gave me a false sense of control, even though the subsequent guilt of premarital sex, which went against everything I had been taught, overwhelmed the temporary solution promiscuity provided. I didn't feel I deserved a good relationship and constantly settled for less. I know now that I was trying to experience the kind of love that I desperately needed.

Once I got married, I tried to block out the rape completely, but my controlling behaviors continued to dictate how I interacted with my husband and handled situations. It wasn't as apparent—once I was married, I stopped being promiscuous—but I wanted control over every aspect of my destiny. I became anxious in the pursuit of my dreams because I couldn't always know what would happen next.

I didn't even like surprise gifts and once argued with my husband for giving me a pair of diamond earrings instead of purchasing a new living room set or some other big-ticket item the whole family could enjoy! Though Elton likes surprises himself, I always insisted that he tell me what he wanted for his birthday or Christmas; I thought I was giving him control, as I would have wanted. This eventually led to less giving and receiving between us—and complacency in the romance department.

During the women's conference, I realized that there was still some residue from the rape and that God wanted to complete the healing process. When the speaker said that I needed to have faith to wait in the dark, I realized that I had to be comfortable with the reality that I wouldn't be able to control everything. If I truly wanted to live a life that was pleasing to God, I would need to walk by faith and not by sight. I would need to embrace and trust God through the unknown—through the things I couldn't control. Though I was trying to protect myself, it didn't make sense to build a wall around me to keep from being wronged again. I needed to be free, believing that if I ever found myself hurt, God had me and could make me whole again.

We are unique beings and instinctively respond to circumstances in our own way, but the Word of God tells us how to handle situations where we've been wronged and need to recover. In my confusion, I had desperately resorted to coping mechanisms that were counterproductive to my recovery. However, in order to reassert the proper measure of control, I needed to acknowledge victory over the situation and bring my thought life, will, emotions, and belief system into alignment with one another.

The law of sin and death had governed my world, and as a result I had carried the shame and burden of rape for a very long time. That burden was lifted when I received the message of Romans 8:1–2. It explains that there is no condemnation (guilt) for those who are in Christ Jesus, because the law of the Spirit of Life has set us free from the law of sin and death. Once I received God into my life, this law set me free in every sense of the word.

I finally concluded that on the night of my rape, I'd had the right to say no at any stage, and the rapist should have stopped. He didn't. I had nothing to be ashamed of. I'd been violated and wronged, but it didn't have to stay that way. I deserved to be loved and treated kindly. My past no longer defined me; it was okay for me to renew my mind in any area of my life, and seek change. For starters, I decided I would appreciate unexpected gifts and let my husband know we needed to reinstate that culture in our home. My husband was pleasantly surprised by the bolder and more assertive Chantale, who expected more of him and more out of life.

Some might read my story and assume there should have been no mercy for a fornicator, for someone who indulged in the lusts of the flesh, for someone who wasn't in a relationship with Christ. But worst-case scenario, even if I were to blame, Jesus took it to the cross and pinned it there. I'm faultless and forgiven! God loved the world (including you and me) so much that He gave His only Son so that when we believe in Him, we won't suffer death, whether emotional or spiritual, but have eternal, unbroken life. When we accept Jesus Christ as our ruler and savior, our victory is assured over the darkness that wants to encroach on our minds and thoughts. Jesus came to redeem those who were under the law, so that we might be adopted as sons and daughters of God by faith (Gal. 4:5, Gal. 3:26). Because of His sacrifice we have the opportunity to be new creations, with our past behind us and a mission before us to tell others of this wonderful gift (2 Cor. 5:7–18).

As I became more familiar with what the Bible said about me, my inner turmoil subsided and I was able to quickly recognize negative, intrusive thoughts and exercise my will based on my renewed belief system instead. I realized that the forces of evil were pleased when I identified as a victim. Proverbs 18:21 tells us that life and death are in the power of the tongue. The words we attribute to ourselves have the power to uplift or destroy our lives. In order to be truly free, I needed to replace the idea of being a victim with the truth of who I really was.

Rape is horrific, but God promises that in all these things we are more than conquerors through Him who loved us. It doesn't matter how terrible our experience was; we are promised victory through our Lord Jesus Christ in 1 Corinthians 15:57. Therefore, I am and you are victorious. That's the identity we should take on.

Still, although we are champions, there's a natural tendency to want an explanation for anything that happens to us. As an auditor, I am trained to ask why until I receive a reasonable answer, until I know exactly what recommendations to make to resolve a problem, and until I determine who is responsible for fixing it. Even as a child, I remember my incessant why in response to whatever answers my parents or other authority figures would give.

So it's not surprising that I would ask why this happened to me. It wasn't the kind of question I could shrug off as unimportant. The problem was that I—like many who have been raped—was only having that dialogue with myself. This left room for me to take the blame, since the predator wasn't assuming responsibility, and there was no objective third party to give the right perspective.

The rapist has his side and I have my side, but God knows and is the truth. 1 John 3:20 says that whenever our hearts condemn us, God is greater than our hearts because He knows everything. Thank God that He is greater than my heart. My heart threw me under the bus even when I was wronged.

And God, knowing the truth, knowing everything from the beginning to the end, pointed out in His Word that we will have tribulations, but that we can take heart because He has overcome the world (John 16:33). Plain and simple, there is evil in this world.

The answer is not more complicated than that.

But greater is He that is in us than he who is in the world (1 John 4:4). We are from God and have overcome these dark rulers and authorities and put them to open shame, through Christ (Col. 2:15). The enemy orchestrates evil deeds because he's always looking for someone to destroy, and one way he tries to trap us is by encouraging us to replay traumatic events in our minds long after they're over. Therefore, we must be watchful that we don't fall prey to the war being waged on our minds (1 Peter 5:8).

Relying on our own understanding can lead us to perpetual despair. Instead we must let peace rule in our hearts (John 16:33), trusting God and allowing the living water—the Word of God—to quench our thirst for answers. It takes self-control not to drive ourselves into depression because our why hasn't been satisfied, but if we take on what the Word of God says, we will be set free (John 8:31–32). Will the images of rape and abuse be seared into our minds for the rest of our lives? How much time is too long to mull over traumatic events? That answer is really up to us.

Hebrews 13:8 says that there should be a consistency that runs through us all, and Jesus is our greatest example of this—He remains the same yesterday, today, and forever. The only thing we should allow to transform us is the word of God, which promises us the spirit of power, love, and a sound mind (2 Tim. 1:7). The Amplified version substitutes "a sound mind" with "self-control." We should love ourselves enough to control our thought life; if we don't exercise this power, we may become paranoid, depressed, or even suicidal.

Embracing what God does for us is the best thing we can do for Him and for us. It's easy to become so well-adjusted to our internal culture that we fit into it without even thinking. When we fix our attention on God instead, we'll be changed from the inside out. We'll readily recognize what He wants from us and quickly respond to it.

Philippians 4:8 says, "Finally, brethren, whatever is true, whatever is honorable, whatever is right, whatever is pure, whatever is lovely, whatever is of good repute, if there is any excellence and anything worthy of praise, dwell on these things" (NASB). We also read in Philippians 4:9 that we must practice these things that we have learned, heard, and seen, not simply for the sake of following the rules, but so that the God of peace can be with us. When we keep our thoughts pure, it's difficult to simultaneously entertain the negativity that can skew our perspective of the precious life we've been given. After all, peace of mind is what matters most after such an ordeal.

Even when rapists haven't been convicted, they are not free or at peace unless they've repented of their wrongdoing and received forgiveness from God. We, on the other hand, have a promise from God that we will not be crushed—even when we are afflicted in every way. We may be full of unanswered questions, but not driven to despair (2 Cor. 4:8).

It requires childlike faith to trust God at His word, but there's no point in knowing that God is able to do exceedingly and abundantly above all that we can think of if we don't believe enough to ask for His help. When we believe, our inner turmoil can subside because of the quiet assurance that we're going to be okay. In fact, God promises that we'll be healthy and full of life when we trust Him with all we have (Prov. 3:5–12).

When we place faith in what He says, we don't

need to know every detail before proceeding, but can trust that He'll guide us at every turn. I love how the story of Jacob demonstrates that God doesn't change. After many years of turmoil with his father-in-law, Jacob made this observation to Rachel and Leah:

> "I notice that your father has changed toward me; he doesn't treat me the same as before. But the God of my father hasn't changed; he's still with me. You know how hard I've worked for your father. Still, your father has cheated me over and over, changing my wages time and again. But God never let him really hurt me. If he said, 'Your wages will consist of speckled animals' the whole flock would start having speckled lambs and kids. And if he said, 'From now on your wages will be streaked animals' the whole flock would have streaked ones. Over and over God used your father's livestock to reward me" (Gen. 31:4–9 MSG).

In this story we see a man who was afflicted but not crushed. In fact, he started to notice a pattern in God's behavior: every time he was aggrieved, God came through for him. What was supposed to destroy him God used for his good. Eventually Jacob's questions triggered instructions for him to move from where he was being abused to a place where God had a different plan for his life.

Sometimes we may feel like our situation is unique and therefore isolates us from the rest of the world. But the things we go through are common to the human experience. Many more before us have handled hardship and abuse at the hands of another; God had a plan and instructions for them, and God has a plan and instructions for us too.

The key is to place our life in God's hands, as instructed in Romans 12:2. With God's help we can take "[our] everyday, ordinary life—[our] sleeping, eating, going-to-work, and walking-around life—and place it before God as an offering" (MSG). A good plan of action may start something like David's in 2 Samuel 12:20: he "got up from the floor, washed his face and combed his hair, put on a fresh change of clothes, then went into the sanctuary and worshiped.

Then he came home and asked for something to eat. They set it before him and he ate" (MSG).

Jesus is in touch with our realities. He's been through weakness and testing, experienced it all—all but the sin. He is prepared to have mercy on us and provide help in every situation. He even taught us how to simply pray. I love The Message translation of the Lord's Prayer in Matthew 6:7–13.

> Our Father in heaven,
> Reveal who you are.
> Set the world right;
> Do what's best—
> as above, so below.
> Keep us alive with three square meals.
> Keep us forgiven with you and forgiving others.
> Keep us safe from ourselves and the Devil.
> You're in charge!
> You can do anything you want!
> You're ablaze in beauty!
> Yes. Yes. Yes.

That chapter continues to explain the connection

between what God does and what we do (Matt. 6:14–15). The gospel of Mark provides additional guidance:

> "Truly I tell you, whoever says to this mountain, Be lifted up and thrown into the sea! and does not doubt at all in his heart but believes that what he says will take place, it will be done for him. For this reason I am telling you, whatever you ask for in prayer, believe (trust and be confident) that it is granted to you, and you will [get it]. And whenever you stand praying, if you have anything against anyone, forgive him and let it drop (leave it, let it go), in order that your Father who is in heaven may also forgive you your [own] failings and shortcomings and let them drop" (Mark 11:23–26 AB).

Our focus should be on the promises meant to sustain us during difficult times rather than on withholding grace from our enemies. The man who raped me didn't stop me from leaving once he got what he wanted; he never called or apologized, even after running into me at an event. He was with someone else. I'm sure a lot has happened in his life since then. For all I know, he may have repented sometime afterward. Nonetheless, forgiving him sets me free and sets me up for success in my prayer life.

Christ died for everyone. When we look at people from this perspective, we'll realize that no matter what someone has done to us, we must look beyond outward appearances and search their hearts. Does Christ live there? Did that person get a fresh start this morning? Did they tap into God's mercies that are new every day? Are they a friend of God? There's no point in maintaining unforgiveness in our hearts for someone who may have received forgiveness already from God. Some may not ask us for forgiveness. Others may have repented long after they knew how to reach us. But when we consider that God thought them precious enough to send His Son to die for them … well, it's time to let it go (2 Cor. 5:14–20).

We can't get forgiveness from God without also forgiving others. When we withhold our forgiveness, God's part is also withheld. We cannot be in faith to move mountains if we stand in prayer with unforgiveness in our hearts. It may seem like the hardest thing to do, but it's the one thing we can't afford to avoid.

Ephesians 6: 10–18 says,

> Finally, be strong in the Lord and in the strength of his might. Put on the whole armor of God, that you may be able to stand against the schemes of the devil. For we do not wrestle against flesh and blood, but against the rulers, against the authorities, against the cosmic powers over this present darkness, against the spiritual forces of evil in the heavenly places. Therefore take up the whole armor of God, that you may be able to withstand in the evil day, and having done all, to stand firm. Stand therefore, having fastened on the belt of truth, and having put on the breastplate of righteousness, and, as shoes for your feet, having put on the readiness given by the gospel of peace. In all circumstances take up the shield of faith, with which you can extinguish all the flaming darts of the evil

> one; and take the helmet of salvation, and
> the sword of the Spirit, which is the word
> of God, praying at all times in the Spirit,
> with all prayer and supplication (ESV).

The efforts we make to recover when we've been wronged can't be done with our own strength or power, but through the Holy Spirit (Zech. 4:6). Even as we suffer from the trauma of our experiences, the blood of Jesus is available for our healing! Jesus may have shed His blood a long time ago, but it never loses its power. No matter what we've been through, our pain can find purpose when we realize that Christ is leading us victoriously through our trials while showing others what's possible through Him (2 Cor. 2:14). The speaker whose story triggered a transformation in my life shared her triumph through Christ, and I now share mine. We don't celebrate what happened, but we can rejoice in how we overcame through Christ who strengthened us (Phil. 4:13). We have conquered by the blood of the Lamb and by the word of our testimonies (Rev. 12:11). This is the victory we have in Jesus!

Childlike Faith Exercises

Who does God say you are? Write out what God says about you, and periodically refer to it for encouragement. Keep in mind that you are not what happened to you, but rather who God says you are.

Do you take the blame for what happened to you in the past? Write down the blame you've placed on yourself, then dispose of it.

Do you have recurring thoughts or images of incidents where you've been hurt? List those images and negative thoughts; then for each one choose a corresponding pure thought that you will think of instead whenever the negative thought surfaces. Dispose of the list of images or negative thoughts once you've created your list of pure thoughts.

Have you been hurt in any way and struggle to forgive? List the people who have hurt you, and release them by faith of their offenses.

Do you have unanswered prayers that may have been hindered because of unforgiveness? Write out your requests so you can remember what's at stake if you find it difficult to forgive.

Pray the Lord's Prayer out loud, and personalize it.

Insert the name(s) of those whom you need to forgive. For example: *Keep me forgiven with You and forgiving* _____.

Prayer

Father in heaven, I thank You for all that You've revealed today. You know me so well and know exactly what I need to complete my healing. Thank You for Your love, grace, and mercy. I receive forgiveness from You, Lord, and forgive everyone who's hurt me. Help me to leave the past behind me and to recognize the effects of dragging the past into the future. I submit my thought life to You and will resist the urge to dwell on negative thoughts. I claim victory in this area of forgiveness, in the name of Jesus. Amen! I give You all the honor!

Chapter 3

God's Promise

The day I met Elton, he told me he would make me his queen. It was our first duty station—Fort Lewis, Washington (now Joint Base Lewis-McChord). My girlfriend, Denise, and her boyfriend, Carvin, had set us up on a blind date. They'd decided I needed to meet one of Carvin's friends so we could double-date.

The day Elton and I were first supposed to meet, something came up and I canceled, thinking nothing of it. What I didn't realize was that Elton took it personally—even though I'd never met him and didn't know what he looked like.

A few weeks later, we were in Carvin's barracks when Elton showed up in a muscle shirt, basketball shorts, and flip-flops because he didn't know I was there. Although he had agreed to the first blind date, our friends didn't dare bring up the possibility of us trying to connect again—they knew he had pretty much written me off for canceling the first date. Instead they conspired to make it seem like happenstance. Just as fast as I could soak in his fresh cut, six-pack, huge biceps, pretty feet for a man, and Carvin's introduction, Elton interrupted to say, "I thought *she* didn't want to meet me!"

"Hello, I have a name." I was furious and suddenly realized why my mom had hated to hear her kids refer to her as "she." "This was not my idea," I said when he simply ignored me. He still didn't respond. Finally I shouted, "Does it look like I can't find a date on my own?" I flared my arms in an hourglass figure and scowled at him.

Carvin and Denise worked to calm us down, and we decided not to ruin the night for everyone. Elton went back to his room and got dressed for the house party we were going to crash. When he came back, he looked even more amazing than before, and I wavered between total infatuation and the memory of just how nasty he had been.

I was still a little indifferent until I heard that a girl I couldn't stand was asking about him. She and I had history. Before I'd joined my unit, all the single soldiers had their own rooms, but my arrival had meant someone had to share. She had told my new roommate, right in front of me, that she would have died if it were her—and how sorry she was for the other girl. When I heard she was trying to figure out if Elton was at the party with anyone, I realized it was the perfect time for me to get revenge. For all she knew, Elton and I had been together forever, given the way I showered him with attention.

I set out to make her jealous. I don't know if it worked, but I didn't give it much thought after that—Elton was turning out to be pretty interesting. When I found out he'd joined the army about a year before I had, on my birthday, that was all I needed to know. I thought he was a Jamaican rude boy as we gyrated to the dancehall and reggae songs, and pretty soon we were dancing closely to Lauryn Hill singing "Killing Me Softly with His Song" as I sang it in his ear. He said he would make me his queen. It sounded good, and I believed him.

Within hours I was in his arms, doing what I had no business doing. After that we couldn't get enough of each other—until two months later, when we found out I was two months pregnant.

I was terrified. I wasn't sure if I could still be in the army as a pregnant, unmarried soldier. I would need a family care plan. I knew no one at Fort Lewis. I finally had health care, so why wasn't I on some kind of birth control? My mind was reeling.

Elton said he wasn't ready to be a father; he wanted to do things the right way. Fine time to make that decision! He would pay for the abortion, he told me. He still wanted to be with me, but this was too much.

I called my mother, who begged me not to go through with it. She offered to take the baby after delivery so I could go on with my life. Elton wouldn't hear of it, and all I could think of was a future filled with the worry and grief of being a single parent. Eventually our selfishness clouded our judgment. We committed to having the abortion.

We set up an appointment for a week or two later. Elton came with me to the clinic and into the room, and we watched as the nurse or the doctor—I couldn't tell you anything about the procedure— vacuumed our baby right out of our lives, forever. Problem solved, right? Wrong!

Depression followed. I was no longer the fun person I'd been, but a guilt-ridden girlfriend clinging to some semblance of control. He dumped me a few weeks later. I desperately tried to hold on to the relationship; I showed up to his barracks unannounced a few days after the breakup, only to realize that he was headed out on another double date with Carvin. I was wearing the comfortable outfit I'd been advised to wear on the day of the abortion. It was the only thing I had left to remind me of my baby. He didn't notice. I was left to grieve alone and full of regret.

The months that followed were a blur of making up, breaking up, and making up again, and crying and expressing regret for what we had done. Eventually I realized I couldn't do this anymore. Operation Move On took a couple of paychecks and included new jeans, new blouses, new shoes, and the famous Halle Berry haircut of the nineties. I bought a VCR and a membership to Blockbuster, a video rental company. Sex would no longer be my pastime; I would catch up on all the movies I hadn't been allowed to watch as a kid.

The problem was that no matter how many times I

read the instructions, I couldn't get the VCR to work. Against my better judgment I called Elton; I still considered him a friend because I had rationalized his behavior. Surprisingly, he said he could fix it if I picked him up.

Well, it turned out I wasn't as technically challenged as I'd thought. Elton glanced at the myriad of cords behind the television and told me I'd managed to not plug in the VCR. I was feeling pretty dumb! I didn't want to drive him home right away, so I invited him to stay and watch the movie I'd planned for that afternoon, *Any Given Sunday* with LL Cool J. I can't remember if we actually watched it, though, because one thing led to another, and I was with him again. It wasn't what I'd expected, but I was so happy he was giving the relationship another chance. Outside of our relationship drama, he was such good company and a great listener.

Weeks later, he got orders to Germany and suggested we get married so we could go together. This certainly took me by surprise; I knew he enjoyed being around me, but it was only implied, never expressed in such a way that a proposal would seem inevitable.

It wasn't exactly the proposal I had envisioned as a young girl, either—there was no ring and no bended knee, no fancy candlelight dinner, or anything else I had imagined. Here he was asking me the most important question after "Will you accept Jesus into your life?" and I had to wonder if he was teasing, because we really didn't have the foundation to warrant such a leap.

In fact, I was so unsure of his sincerity that I attempted to call his bluff. I don't think I actually said yes. I do remember saying, "If you're serious, let's go get the rings now." Apparently he was serious; we went to a local jewelry store, purchased our rings in a package deal, and got engaged that day. The following day we went to the courthouse to get our marriage license and found out we still had to wait three days before we could get married.

Our sudden engagement wasn't well received by our families—especially his. I remember his twin sister asking him to check under his bed for some sort of talisman that I might have used to bewitch him into marriage. She knew I was of Haitian descent, and she seemed to be implying I'd used voodoo to trick him. Another family member thought the separation could help us determine if it were truly meant to be.

Perhaps it was a good thing that they didn't agree. Now it was us against the world, and the opposition deepened our bond. Despite their advice, we got married on July 9, 1999—the day after my birthday—on our lunch break, in our fatigues, at a love chapel because the courthouse was booked. Only one guest attended: Denise, who'd introduced us.

Elton seemed sincere about wanting to do things the right way, and I decided that our breakups and makeups were simply the growing pains of our relationship. I was ready to put the past behind me, especially the nightmare of the abortion.

But I couldn't forget about her. I didn't exactly know that our baby was a girl, but in my heart I had named her Christina. Once in a while Elton and I would look at each other with regret, wondering why we'd had the abortion since we ended up getting married anyway. At other times I questioned his love for me, certain that he'd only married me out of guilt. What made matters worse was that several years later we had difficulty getting pregnant.

Month after month passed before we decided to see a specialist, who told us Elton could populate the earth. The problem was me. I simply wasn't very fertile; it would take careful planning and perfect timing for me to get pregnant.

The doctor saw me for several days until an ultrasound revealed that my eggs were ready, and then he told us to go home and do the deed. We were ecstatic when we found out about a month later that I was pregnant—with twins! The timing was right. I was getting out of the army, and we were scheduled to return to the United States after being stationed in Germany for three years. It was finally time to have a family.

In our last few months in Germany, we caught up on all the sightseeing we should have been doing the whole time we'd been there. I puked in Paris, I puked in Spain, and I puked in Prague. I don't know what I was thinking. When we got to Fort Hood, we put in fourteen-hour days looking at houses and then apartments. Finally we decided to build instead. When we had a moment to breathe, I realized I missed seeing my babies on the regular ultrasounds I'd had with the specialist in Germany. We hadn't even been assigned a new doctor yet.

I told Elton that I wanted to go to the emergency

room so they could check on the babies, so we came up with a story about blood on my underwear. Little did I know that I was four centimeters dilated and in the process of miscarrying. We were only a few days shy of five months pregnant.

I couldn't believe I was losing my babies. We asked every question we could think of to every medical professional who came to our room, but there was nothing they could do to stop it from happening. We didn't know God for ourselves; we didn't know of His undying love and mercy. I'd like to think that if I'd known God like I do now, I wouldn't have lost the babies. Instead I was so guilt-ridden from the abortion that I thought it was payback or punishment. A chaplain representative came to pray with us, but we didn't know about having faith for a miraculous intervention. We were too overcome with shame and self-condemnation.

Our son Christopher was born three days before his twin brother, Xavier. Christopher lived for an hour, and when he was born I watched my husband crazily reach for an oxygen tank in the room, yelling at the doctors that surely there was something they could do. I held my baby close and cried silent tears.

My husband is a twin. This was devastating for him.

Somehow we still hoped that our second baby would live, but after I'd been in the hospital for seven days, Xavier was born. Stillborn. I held him even tighter than I had held his brother. He had been my last hope. We were crushed.

Even though I had felt regret over the abortion, it took the loss of my twins for me to realize just how precious life is. Here I was pro-choice, thinking I was controlling my future, but I didn't really have a choice now. I wasn't in control at all. We'd taken it for granted that we could just have a baby when we were good and ready, but we were wrong.

In the months that followed, Elton and I became distant. We handled our grief differently and apart. I couldn't shake the questions that kept flooding my mind. When had I become this person? How had I ended up with Elton? We'd lost our babies, and all he wanted to do was hang out with his motorcycle club. The most talking we did was knowing looks.

We were only at Fort Hood for five months before Elton was deployed to Iraq for a year. He didn't get to experience us closing on our first home. For me it was bittersweet; we had built this four-bedroom home for the twins, but now I was moving into it by myself. Everything happened fast, and then there was silence. I was left alone with my regret, guilt, and shame.

By the time Elton returned from his deployment, our pain had been swept under the rug, though not forgotten. We got pregnant as soon as he got home. This time I was considered a high-risk pregnancy, so the doctors monitored me closely. Turns out I had an incompetent cervix; sure enough, right around the same time I'd lost the twins, my body started to reject the baby again. The doctors caught it in time to put in a cerclage to stitch my cervix shut. I had to be on bed rest the entire pregnancy. I was so miserable that I continued my degree online during that time, just to avoid going crazy.

Our beautiful, smart, funny daughter was born on Christmas Eve. She had a head full of hair and looked like a doll. With all the time on my hands before she was born, I had researched the perfect name to capture her essence. Vivianna with two n's—full of life and full of grace. She gave me renewed purpose, responsibility, joy, and love. Life wasn't exactly perfect, but I had hope, and at least I felt forgiven.

For the first time in years, I acknowledged God and gave thanks.

I had thought having our daughter would slow my husband down or at least help me not miss him as much, but it didn't. It wasn't long before Elton was back to his old ways and then on another tour to Iraq, and even more distant than before. Part of me didn't think I deserved better. How could I complain? I'd slept with him on the first night. I'd had an abortion. He would never respect or value me. I'd made my bed and let him lie in it. We didn't know what love was. I didn't know who I was. I just knew I had a daughter I wanted so much more for. I cried a desperate prayer.

Even though I now had a child, my abortion continued to haunt me. I remember going to a doctor once to evaluate whether my incompetent cervix was a service-connected disability. That was the worst appointment I'd ever had. He began by asking routine questions about my medical history, but he quickly ended the evaluation when I told him about the abortion. "What did you expect after getting something like that done?" the doctor asked. It didn't matter that I'd had other invasive procedures too. He didn't hear me out. It was my first time sharing this with a stranger, and I was flooded with guilt all over again.

That day I realized I had developed the habit of using food for comfort. I had a sudden craving for a specific cheesecake from a fast-food joint. I'd always been able to appease my cravings so quickly that I didn't realize they were an addiction. On this particular day they'd run out of the cheesecake, and I drove to several locations, feeling crazy because I couldn't find it. This wasn't a pregnancy craving; this was a longing in my soul for something of substance to fill it. I'd thought my husband would do that; I'd thought my daughter would do that; I'd thought my degree would do that. Something. Anything. Realizing I was empty scared me. I cried some more. I stopped telling doctors I'd had an abortion. I couldn't stand the possible judgment.

I don't know what cries tugged at God's heartstrings, but as I was trying to figure out how to leave Elton while he was deployed, I got the phone call telling me he'd gotten saved—he had given his life to Jesus. I didn't know what to think, but in the end I chose to give this new lifestyle a chance. It was the best decision I'd ever made. Surrendering my life to God gave Him access to mend every area of my life that had been broken through my own actions or the negligence of others.

Shortly after Elton dedicated his life to God, he called me from Iraq and told me he wanted to have another child. "God spoke to me and told me that I would have a son," he said. He wanted me to get pregnant when he came home for his R&R (rest and relaxation) break midway through his deployment.

I thought he was crazy. Here he was just a few months with Jesus, and all of a sudden he was deep enough to hear from God. I figured the biblical story of Abraham had given him this bright idea. I also thought he was selfish. How dare he ask me to get pregnant again, when he wouldn't even be there during the toughest part! Imagine being on bed rest with a toddler at home! Our beautiful daughter was worth the sacrifice, pain, and suffering, but I was too afraid to go through something like that again. Besides the stress of hoping to get pregnant in only two weeks, the mental agony, the fear of it all being in vain, was enough for me to flat-out refuse.

My husband didn't argue, but simply restated that

God had told him he would have a son. In the days that followed, my heart softened to the idea—but I wouldn't budge in my resolve. Getting pregnant under those conditions was too much to ask. However, God has an amazing way of turning hearts and orchestrating opportunities to be in faith.

I remember the day my mindset shifted. During praise and worship our pastor sang, "We prepare the way, we prepare the way, we prepare the way of the Lord" over and over again. The planned order of service was obviously being thrown out the window. The atmosphere had changed, and it was like nothing I had ever experienced.

She said the Holy Spirit was in the place. I knew of the Holy Spirit, but never had I experienced His presence to the point where I felt I could reach out and grab it. She said there was healing, and frankly, it didn't matter what was being offered—I wanted some of it.

I joined the group of people hurrying to the altar and watched in fascination and adoration all at once. Something supernatural was taking place, though it was something I knew nothing of. I watched as the pastor placed her hands on each person's head as she prayed for them, and I put my hands up and joined in worship—"We prepare the way, we prepare the way, we prepare the way of the Lord"—watching as she made her way toward me.

What happened next blew me away. Instead of touching my head, she placed her hand on my belly and began to pray. In that instant I knew I would have a child, and that it would be a boy. My pregnancy would be flawless, and I would get pregnant during the two weeks that my husband was on R&R.

I had only been attending my church for about six months. No one knew me or knew my story. My husband had never even been there, but I couldn't wait to contact him and let him know I was in. We were going to have a baby!

Elton was scheduled to come home for R&R in July for my birthday and our anniversary. We made all sorts of plans for this awesome two weeks of baby-making; I even scheduled a doctor's appointment to take a pregnancy test about a month after he was supposed to be home. But July came and went; his R&R kept getting postponed because terrorists were targeting flights.

He finally made it home on August 1, and we went to the doctor's appointment anyway and talked about our plans to get pregnant. After asking a few questions about my last cycle and my medical history, the doctor announced that it was the perfect time for Elton and I to have sex. I was in my ovulation window; had Elton come home any sooner, his little soldiers would have gone to waste.

God's timing is impeccable. Like my senior pastor used to say, delay does not mean denial. All things work together for our good. Elton's R&R rotation was the first to go from fourteen to eighteen days. On August 12 we were baptized and became members of our church, beginning the greatest adventure of our lives. On August 15 I took an early pregnancy test that came back positive. Pregnant in two weeks! We had tried for years before we became pregnant with the twins. This was surely a miracle.

Elton continued to pray and declare that we would be victorious. Although my doctors monitored me closely because of my medical history, I had a smooth pregnancy. The doctors said my cervix might need stitching, but it never got to that point; I even worked up until a week before the baby was born. We were overjoyed when an ultrasound confirmed the sex of our baby. God was faithful in His promise. We were having a boy: Elton B. Williams Jr. I wanted him to have faith like Daddy.

In that moment, God touched me in an area of my life where I was still guilt-ridden from the abortion and feeling unworthy of His favor. I finally felt forgiven and empowered to do things God's way through faith.

Childlike Faith Exercises

Are you in faith for a child? What God did for me, He can do for you. He is still performing the baby-making miracles of Bible days, and the same power that was available then is available now. I am in faith with you for God's promise to manifest in your life, in Jesus' name. It doesn't matter how long you've been trying. Renew your faith today for your baby, your bundle of joy.

Have you lost a child during pregnancy and sometimes feel hopeless? God will restore what the enemy stole. Even though Vivianna and Elton Jr. didn't replace our lost twins, now that we know God we can rest assured that we will one day be reunited with Christopher and Xavier—and meet Christina, too. I pray that the same peace we have rules in your heart and that your hope is restored in Jesus' name.

Do you feel undeserving of God's mercy because of your past, and as a result you don't pray boldly in faith for the promises God made available to you? If you haven't already repented, repent now and receive His forgiveness and forgive yourself. Leave your past behind you, in faith, and know that God wants your relationship with Him restored through Christ Jesus and is prepared to shower you with gifts reserved especially for you.

Prayer

Dear God,

You are such a forgiving and loving Father. I thank You now for Your mercy toward me. Lord, Your ways are higher than my ways, and Your thoughts are higher than my thoughts. I'm grateful that You remain on the throne no matter what is going on. May Your marvelous kingdom and Your will be established here on earth and specifically in my life.

Father, You know my needs and my desires, and I trust You as my source, as the giver of life. Forgive me for my sins—the ones I know of, the ones I don't know of, and the ones whose magnitude I can't even comprehend. Help me to forgive myself and forgive those I've allowed to hurt me and those I couldn't stop if I wanted to. I put them all in Your hands now. Help me to uphold my values and Your ways during moments of temptation. Lord, I come boldly before You in faith for Your promises for my life. In the mighty name of Jesus. Amen.

Chapter 4

Transparent Transgressions

When Elton and I were baptized and joined our church, we began a most amazing journey of restoration, faith, and growth. But receiving Christ into our lives didn't mean we wouldn't face difficulties. In fact, Jesus tells us in John 16:33, "In the world you have tribulation and distress and suffering, but be courageous [be confident, be undaunted, be filled with joy]; I have overcome the world" (AB). Jesus deprived it of the power to harm us, and He conquered it for us. Through these trials we have the opportunity to exercise our faith in His promises and have confidence and peace in Him. Often our greatest victories come in the middle of our greatest trials.

Well, just as the Word warned, we did experience trials. About two years later, Elton got orders to go back to Fort Lewis, Washington. It was the worst possible timing. I had recently quit my job to start a business. We were active in our local church and felt like we were too new at this God thing to separate ourselves from that particular body of believers and spiritual leaders. We were in faith that the orders would be reversed, but a few days before his report date we finally acknowledged the inevitable. He packed his car and drove to Fort Lewis, all the while believing that God would make a way.

That eighteen-month separation took a toll on our marriage and our finances, and the situation made us question our faith. But what the enemy meant for evil would turn out for our good in the most unlikely way.

I remember trying to reach Elton one night and not being able to get through. During our first two years after being saved, we'd felt we could conquer the world together, but this night something seemed off. Mistrust seeped into my being. Where was he? Why wasn't he answering my calls? This was not like the new Elton. All I could think of was the insensitive Elton, who once dumped me to prove to his friends that he wasn't wrapped around my finger. I imagined the worst and even assumed that he was up to his old ways.

In the past I would already have launched a full-on investigation into his whereabouts and cracked every password to his bank accounts, email, and phone—whatever helped me figure out where he was and whom he was with. It's what we often do when we suspect a loved one is cheating. We lose clear thinking and common sense. Our soul feels like it's dying. We get tired and start mentally tripping, imagining crazier and crazier scenarios. We can't sleep, so we snoop. We panic and attack the pantry. We react rather than respond to the situation.

The mistrust and anxiety that were brewing were familiar; this was how I always had reacted to his behavior. But I didn't like how it felt now, and what it could mean. Fear is not attractive. It attempts to destroy the belief that we are made in the image and likeness of God—full of power and control. Fear breeds insecurity, an equally unattractive trait that repels the people we love and need around us. I remember telling God that I didn't get saved to be going through this kind of emotional turmoil.

That night I simply wanted peace in the middle of my doubts and fears. I wanted to cast my cares on Him. This is what I had been learning for the past two years, and the hope that it had instilled was transformative; I didn't want to go back. God reminded me of His promise in Proverbs 3:24: "If you lie down, you will not be afraid; when you lie down, your sleep will be sweet" (ESV). That's exactly what I needed—to sleep without anxiety for Elton's phone call or explanation.

I love The Message version of this Scripture because it captures what I could have put myself through if I hadn't prayed for sweet sleep. It says,

> Dear friend, guard Clear Thinking and
> Common Sense with your life;
> don't for a minute lose sight of them.
> They'll keep your soul alive and well,
> they'll keep you fit and attractive.
> You'll travel safely,
> you'll neither tire nor trip.
> You'll take afternoon naps without a worry,
> you'll enjoy a good night's sleep.
> No need to panic over alarms or surprises,

or predictions that doomsday's just around the
corner,
Because God will be right there with you;
he'll keep you safe and sound (Prov. 3:21–26).

God is faithful to His promise. Within minutes I
was in a sleep so deep that when the phone rang, I
was surprised that only fifteen minutes had gone by.
Elton said that he had taken an early nap after going
to the sauna in preparation for a physical training test
the following day; he had just noticed the missed
phone calls when he woke. At that moment I was
already overwhelmed with God's peace and simply
wished my husband well on the test. We said our
goodbyes as I dozed off into sweet surrender.

The next morning my sister-in-law, who lived with
me at the time, joined me on a brisk walk around the
school playground across from my home. As we
headed back I sensed that I needed to keep walking
and take advantage of that time to pray for my
husband to do well on the test. However, I felt lazy
and decided to go back inside. When we arrived at my
front door I remember asking my sister-in-law if God
was saying anything to her.

She threw the question back at me, and I admitted that I needed to pray and walk some more. God was urging us both to pray. Neither of us was up for walking another step, but we eventually yielded and began to pray for my husband and pray in the Spirit as we walked. Within twenty minutes we returned home for the second time, and Elton called as we walked up the driveway. My sister-in-law went into the house while I caught a private moment in the garage to talk with Elton about bills and other household issues.

Little did we know that we had just engaged in spiritual warfare. Often God urges us to pray or do something seemingly random that is directly connected to the breakthrough we are seeking in the natural realm. Our obedience that day changed the direction of my life, and I couldn't have orchestrated the victory that followed.

Midway through what I thought was an everyday conversation, my husband blurted out, "You think it's easy for me to say no when somebody says they don't care if I'm married?" Here we were talking about bills, and his real thoughts escaped him out loud. Immediately he tried to shut the conversation down.

"You don't wanna know. You can't handle it!"

I couldn't believe what was happening, but what I said next did not come from the old me. "I'm in a relationship with Jesus Christ! If you think I got saved and He didn't make me strong enough to deal with whatever it is you can't seem to say, then you don't know my God!" I was prepared to face the ugly realities of our marriage, and there was no better time than now.

Elton told me what really had happened the night I couldn't reach him. He was with someone, a one-night stand with an instructor from a military course he was attending. She was only in town for that week and had slipped him her business card with her hotel information scribbled on the back. He'd gone to visit her, all the while making excuses to himself to justify the visit. One thing had led to another, and he had collapsed like a folding chair.

For many years I had pictured what I would do if I caught him or found proof of his cheating. This was nothing like I had imagined. A single tear rolled down my cheek. All those years of holding on, hoping things would change, thinking I was the jealous one— or even paranoid. Now I had a confession, which meant we had a decision to make.

Still in the garage, I sat in my car with the door pushed open so I could breathe, and surrounded by darkness, I asked for honesty. Did he still want to be married to me? If not, there was no point in addressing anything else. He said that he not only wanted our marriage, he wanted us to be right. We must have talked for hours. I didn't make it to work that day. We went through every incident I could remember and every female I had ever suspected him of being with, and each time I asked for the truth. I needed to be able to trust my instincts.

He confessed to them all except one. To my surprise, I realized that the one time I was wrong was the one time I was so exasperated by his behavior that I had cheated on him. Now I almost envied him. Here he was, getting free from his sin while I was still bearing my secret. I was already prepared to forgive him, but would he forgive me? Fear gripped me. I'd always felt there was a double standard when it came to men; the biggest liars and cheaters required the most loyalty.

Just hours earlier I'd told him that God had made me strong enough to deal with whatever he had to say, but now I was afraid to confess. Finally I decided to trust God and shared my secret, hoping my husband would say he still wanted to be married. At first he was silent, and when he spoke, all he could muster was "Wow!"

Eventually he admitted that he was humbled by what I had shared; he would never have suspected that I was capable of doing something like that to him. He realized how foolish he'd been to treat me that way and expect no repercussions. Still, I was apologetic, and we decided that we wanted to work things out.

So we began our journey of transparency and rebuilding trust in our marriage. It was only by the grace of God that we were able to withstand the recovery process and remain accountable to each other. Eventually Elton returned to Texas, and our confessions freed us to pursue our relationship with renewed zest. Now when we meditate on the Word, we are even more convinced that our marriage was and is still worth fighting for.

From the beginning of time, the enemy has attempted to cause strife in the marriage relationship. He has no new tricks. He was deceptive with Eve, and Adam fell for it too. Although our relationship was built on sand, when we accepted Jesus Christ as our Lord and Savior, that sand solidified into rock. We are stronger than ever. God had a plan for our marriage, and He has a plan for yours too.

Some may read this and think we need therapy or that one of us is getting played. Adultery is often the ticket to walk away. But when I think of the love God has for us and the fact that He has never cheated and remains faithful to less than perfect beings, I'm impressed to hold on. Love is not the feeling of butterflies in our stomachs but the ability to see each other as God does and deem each other lovable because God loves us. God's love ensures that "all things work together for good according to his design and purpose" (Rom. 8:28 ESV).

Because we surrendered our lives to God, He stepped into yet another area to make it whole. God wanted more than our future; He wanted to rewrite our perspective of the past. He didn't want our secrets to define us but our confessions to set us free to love unconditionally and without guilt. Our marriage was restored to heavenly dignity.

A few years after Elton returned home from Fort

Lewis, we realized we faced a reassignment. This was a tough pill to swallow. We had been at Fort Hood for ten years by then and had attended our church for seven of those ten years. The thought of leaving turned our world upside down.

Was this move from God? Or was it a distraction we would need to get in a faith fight for? After what we had been through, we knew we would never willingly opt for a separation again. Our pastors encouraged us, telling us we were equipped to transition and that our steps were ordered of the Lord. Still, it was hard to believe that God wanted us anywhere else. So much good had come out of our time in Texas.

We waited a few days to hear the options: Fort Bliss, Texas, and Fort Riley, Kansas. Germany was also a possibility, but we had to wait to find out if that was an option.

Well, it was a no-brainer. If we were going to be uprooted from our comfort zone, it had better be for an assignment worth talking about. We spent the next month on pins and needles waiting to find out, but we were glad we'd held on; we were reassigned to Germany.

Being a military spouse comes with its share of drawbacks, including trying to maintain a career while moving from place to place. One of the incentives I'd had for staying behind when Elton went to Fort Lewis was that I had just started a federal position. This time I wouldn't remain in the United States, but going with Elton could come at a material cost if my job couldn't transfer me.

As we waited for Elton's branch manager to pinpoint the assignment, I found out that the agency I worked for had an office in Wiesbaden, Germany, and that they would gladly relocate me there. Our steps began to look ordered when the branch manager told us Elton's specific assignment was to Wiesbaden. Later I learned that my agency planned to close our office at Fort Hood. God was surely on our side.

The biggest hurdle we faced was the sale of our dream home, purchased just two years earlier. The last thing we wanted was to be stuck with a mortgage or slow-paying renters, but since we hadn't owned the home for a long time, we were afraid we wouldn't be able to sell it for enough to cover a real estate agent's fees, much less make a profit. Elton was adamant that we could sell it ourselves. I was a nervous wreck! We only had a few months, and using a real estate agent could have provided more visibility, but Elton wouldn't budge. Of course I could see the advantage of eliminating the 6 percent fees; on the other hand, it meant we increased the risk of not selling on time. The decision was even more difficult because we knew several Realtors, some of whom were offended that we wouldn't sell through them.

Years before, I had learned to go with Elton's choice when we couldn't agree or when neither option offered guaranteed results. It was at a marriage seminar that I'd picked up this small principle that made a huge difference in my life—though at first I'd had to resist the urge to roll my eyes and suck my teeth when the speaker introduced the Scripture reminding me of my duty to submit. It wasn't the first time that I had heard of wives submitting to their husbands (Eph. 5:22–24); I wanted some other approach to keep my marriage intact.

What she shared instead was a strategy for decision-making between husband and wife. She started off by explaining that in the Christian home, the man was the head of the household. God gave the man specific authority over his home, and as a woman I needed to submit to the will of my husband. She put in the usual disclaimers—not if he's abusive or asking me to violate the Word of God—but other than that, honey, I needed to submit.

I remember thinking of many more ordinary instances where I wouldn't want to submit. My husband has pretty expensive hobbies, and I haven't always been happy with some of his "investments" in top-of-the-line gear. We don't always agree on how to discipline the kids, either. But then she pointed out that even when my husband's final decision seemed ill-advised—or stupid—I was still to submit. She explained that submitting to my husband was like submitting to God's Word even when I don't fully understand His ways. When I submit to God's Word, He is obligated to come through for me. Even if my husband wasn't making what I thought was the best decision for our family, she said, God would come through for us because He would honor my submission.

That resonated with me. It gave me an opportunity to exercise faith in the decision-making process, especially when we were faced with options that weren't necessarily good or bad. It also relieved me of the pressure of determining the best course of action. Sure, I could state my point, but in the end my husband would bear the brunt of the decision.

As women, we sometimes take on more responsibility than we need to. We're like fine china being handled like mugs. When we're confident in who we are, we don't have to prove that we can handle more.

I thought I had checked the block on the submission thing. What I didn't realize was that when I submitted in such a way that my heart was not in it—waiting to see my husband fail or be wrong—I was cheating our relationship of the power of agreement. Agreement is a matter of the heart. We can abide by the terms of the agreement, but the power is unleashed when the hearts are as one.

It seemed like the simplest thing to do, but it was hard work, and our past didn't make the process any easier. However, when we are united there is a greater mystery at work than we can imagine. How we carry out our responsibilities toward each other has the ability to hinder or facilitate our prayers. Believing that God was obligated to make it right for me even if my husband was not as right as he could be made it easier for my heart to jump on board. I knew that when the two of us were of one accord, our plans took on a life of their own and lined up with what heaven had for us.

With that in mind, I reluctantly agreed to place a For Sale by Owner sign in our yard. At first we seemed to have regular traffic and even a serious buyer; then everything went silent for over a month. I became more anxious with every passing day. The clock was ticking. Had we made the right decision? Life was a whirlwind of pre-move preparations: shipping Elton's vehicle and our household goods, booking flights, visiting family, selling my car, relinquishing our ministry duties, attending Elton's graduation, waiting for passports, and hoping that everything would happen in time for us to leave for Germany.

Then at a church service one evening about five weeks before we were scheduled to leave, our pastor spoke prophetically: God would do it again, working miraculously on our behalf as He had in the past. I remember sharing with Elton that even though our pastor was speaking prophetically, I was not comforted by what I'd heard. The last time I'd needed a miracle in a housing situation, God had come through, but it was very uncomfortable—and my miracle didn't come quite like I'd had in mind. Although our pastor was saying what I needed to hear, my focus shifted to the uncertainty that creeps in when I'm trying to walk by faith. I wasn't looking forward to the process.

Still, God appeased my fears through His Word. The following morning I read the story of David slaying Goliath, and it dawned on me that David's confidence in God grew from his previous encounters with the bear and the lion. Had he not experienced them, he would not have had the boldness to ask, "Who is this uncircumcised Philistine that defiles the armies of God?" (1 Samuel 17:26).

I envisioned David struggling to kill the bear and the lion in private as he tended the sheep, and how it probably was nowhere near as sexy as killing Goliath on a world stage, with lives at stake and God's reputation on the line, and in one swoop with a slingshot and a smooth stone. We hear about David's victories with the lion and the bear, but that Goliath victory—now that's a story!

With David's story as the backdrop and the pastor's prophecy echoing in my mind, the Word that was sown took root, the weeds that tried to choke the revelation were suddenly yanked out, and since it was springtime, the Word flourished immediately. I turned to Elton, who was lying beside me, and declared—more like blurted out—"This house sells today!"

In that moment Elton and I were aligned with heaven, my words were aligned with heaven, and the power of agreement was at play. The confidence with which those words came out of my mouth exuded power.

Later that evening Elton called me; someone was interested in seeing the house right away, but he'd told them to come by the next day since he thought I wouldn't want to scramble to get the house ready for showing. On any other day, Elton would have been right. But at that moment I remembered the epiphany I'd had earlier, and I told him to find out whether they still wanted to come that day. They did!

I'd never cleaned so fast in my life. Elton usually does most of the cleaning, but that day I discovered I knew how to clean too. When we met the potential buyers, we clicked like long-lost friends. They loved the house and our furniture, too, and rushed us into contract.

We'd been stationed in Germany once before and knew it was likely our government quarters wouldn't fit all of our belongings, so we'd decided to offer our furniture to whomever would buy our home. These buyers wanted whatever we would leave behind.

The buyers didn't have a real estate agent either and were okay with not including a Realtor on the deal. We had planned to pay an agent to write up the contract for us, but when we tried calling one, we didn't get an answer. We wrote the contract ourselves using our previous home purchase contract as a template.

The next couple of weeks were a race against time. Even though we were under contract, we still had to wait for the different players to do their parts: the appraiser, the home inspector, and then finally the underwriter to make the final review. Our plane tickets were already purchased for June 14. And wouldn't you know it? God did it again! We closed on the sale of our home on June 13 at 11:30 a.m. and received the wire transfer for the balance a couple hours later.

It's funny how hindsight brings so much into perspective. God knew what was ahead—the housing miracle I'd been somewhat disappointed with earlier was just the right house to move quickly when we needed it to.

We boarded our flight as planned, fully persuaded that God was up to something on this next leg of our journey. Our steps were ordered of the Lord (Ps. 37:23), and we gave Him all the glory, honor, and praise. Although we've experienced tribulations and trials, frustrations and distress, we've also experienced newfound heights in our faith walk as we've watched God come through for us in so many different areas of our lives. The same is available to all of His children.

Childlike Faith Exercises

List the trials, tribulations, frustrations, and distress that you are experiencing right now. Find Scriptures that show how God will come through for that particular difficulty. For example, if you are dealing with a health issue, find a Scripture that promises healing. If during your season of trials you find yourself dealing with insomnia, pray for sweet sleep using Proverbs 3:24. For an all-encompassing Scripture you can use John 16:33 and declare that Jesus overcame the issue you are facing, and that with His help you can, too. Believe.

If you're married, purpose in your heart to recognize your husband's headship in spite of what may have happened in the past. Make a conscious effort to do right, and don't let anything terrify you; don't give in to fear or let anxiety discourage you. Operate in the knowledge that you and your spouse are joint heirs of the grace of life and that your prayers can be effective. Find endearing names to call your husband that allude to his authority, and begin to use them regularly.

(1 Peter 3:5–7)

Prayer

Dear God,

I thank You, Lord, for the peace I have in You through Your Son, Jesus Christ. Your Spirit orders my steps, and I have nothing to fear. Thank You, Father, for Your divine order in my life and in my home. I honor my husband today as the leader in our home, as Your Word instructs. Let my marriage be an example of what You want to see here on earth. Equip me to represent You in this world through my marriage. Lord, I forgive my husband and myself for disobeying Your Word, and I ask personally for our forgiveness. We surrender in peace to Your will, and we thank You, Jesus, for having overcome the world. We bask in Your glory. You are an awesome God! In Jesus' name. Amen.

Chapter 5

To Give or not to Give

Like most people, I'm wired to think that someone's out to get my money. As a business major, with marketing at the core of my studies, I know that people are out to get my money. As an auditor, I'm adamant about internal controls to ensure my money is protected from people who are out to get it. Ha!

Imagine my resistance when Elton first told me he needed me to pay his tithes for him while he was deployed. Whoa! My wiring kicked in. *Ding, ding ding, ding, ding, ding ding. Someone's trying to get my money.* Ten percent? What kind of marketing voodoo had this preacher breathed over my newly saved husband? It didn't matter how I worked the math; 100 percent minus 10 percent equals 90 percent, and 90 percent is less than 100 percent.

I'd been told that nothing in life was free and that I had to be willing to give to get. But as an accountant, I knew I had to put money in the right pots if I expected it to all balance out. The bean counter in me didn't think paying tithes was going to add up. I told Elton it was time for him to pump his brakes. He was moving way too fast.

With Elton, though, it was all or nothing. He calmly and politely explained that I could either pay (return, give, sow) his tithes or he could stop sending his direct deposits to our joint account and instead send me a portion of it to cover a share of our living expenses. Oh snap, I guess he told me. New math alert—90 percent was greater than 50 percent. *I'll take it!*

Eventually it dawned on me that God, who had given me life and all my abilities, required only a small percentage in comparison to what He had done for me. It even felt a little silly to negotiate with God on giving 10 percent to advance His kingdom, considering that I would be nothing without Him. I was so convicted that the first tithe I gave was in the middle of the week, during a rare Texas blizzard; I couldn't wait until Sunday to get it done.

Shortly after that, I started tithing on my income as well. We've been tithing and making offerings ever since, and I know that our money has stretched inexplicably compared to when we weren't giving at all.

God wants to bless us financially. He wants to reverse the curses of Genesis 3:16–19 and replant us where He intended for us to prosper (Ps. 1:2–3), blessing us to the point where we don't have room to receive it all (Mal. 3:8–10). He made provisions for a lifestyle of abundance that's connected to serving His kingdom. God wants to ensure that whatever we put our hands to prospers (Ps. 1:3), and that the timing of our endeavors is perfectly in line with the yes of heaven (Ps. 1:3). It pays to serve God and to honor God with our words and actions.

This may seem hard to believe, especially when we see others progressing at record speed without His help—or even by using tactics and strategies that are completely contrary to His Word. While we wait for God's promises and our desires to manifest in our lives, it's tempting to wonder if doing as God says is even possible, let alone reasonable for us.

To naturally lean toward giving over getting and

thereby get what we've been looking for, we can't be worried about missing out. We have to trust that our heavenly Father knows what we need and what concerns us, and that when we give our attention to God and His initiatives, all our needs will be met.

Matthew 6:33 tells us to seek first the kingdom of God and His righteousness, and "all these things" will be given to us. These could be anything that would stop us from focusing on God and doing what is right, including worrying about what the future holds and how we'll make it financially. God reminds us that birds are continually fed, even when they "neither sow nor reap nor gather into barns" and that the lilies of the field are better dressed than king "Solomon in all his magnificence" (Matt. 6:26-29 AB). That passage specifically talks about the worry of what to eat or drink and what to wear, but it also applies to other concerns, like rank or position. We are so much more valuable to God than the birds and the lilies— imagine how much more He will take care of us! This truth must be deeply rooted before we can really be carefree.

Focusing on God is action driven. It's not simply reading the Bible all day and all night and singing

"Kumbaya" until a glory cloud fills our closet. Focusing on God is something that's intended to be part of our daily routine whenever we're faced with opportunities to be and act more like Him. It's making His business a priority in our lives and letting Him take care of the rest as it comes. Whether we find ourselves in situations that we created, circumstances we have no control over, or a combination of the two, God is prepared to give us applicable strategies when we seek Him.

Although this may not come easily, God sees our struggle; He's taking note of our convictions, and He knows our final resolve. The time will come in the middle of the storm when He will take swift action and return the honor we gave His name. At that point all will see the difference between doing the right thing or not, giving or not, serving or not (Mal. 3:17–18). People will see what it's really like to be empowered and happy.

All throughout the Bible, we see God giving people of faith strategies for provision and abundance. I love the story of the widow woman who would have had to sell her sons into slavery if she couldn't pay her debts. She was smart enough to go to the prophet Elisha for advice. Elisha asked her if she had anything of value in her home, but all she had was a single jar of oil. God, through the prophet, told her to borrow empty vessels from all her neighbors and fill the vessels with the little oil she had. As she poured the oil, it multiplied—enough that she was able to sell the full vessels to pay her debts and live off the rest (2 Kings 4:1–7).

In the story of the widow woman, God provided a plan that directly impacted her breakthrough. The story of Joseph is equally compelling because it demonstrates that God also delivers strategies indirectly that yield similar results. When God gave Joseph the ability to interpret Pharaoh's dreams, Joseph realized that Egypt would experience a long famine preceded by many prosperous years. Joseph advised Pharaoh to save a portion of food from the abundant years so Egypt could use the surplus during the famine. This ability to interpret dreams got Joseph out of prison and then put in command over the operation, overseeing the great wealth transfer to Egypt as others gave up their possessions for food. In the process he was also able to help his family. God gave Joseph strategies for others that in turn benefited him as well (Gen. 41).

God is concerned with every aspect of our lives, and He looks out for the little things just as He does the huge financial decisions. Jesus taught Peter that some things we deal with just because we live in this world, while some of our battles position us for victories that serve a greater good for those in our sphere of influence. When Peter was confronted about whether Jesus paid taxes, he could easily have come up with a reason Jesus should have been exempt from taxation. However, taxes were part of the routine. Jesus not only advised Peter to pay the taxes, but made miraculous provision for him to do so. Jesus said, "However, so that we do not offend them, go to the sea and throw in a hook, and take the first fish that comes up; and when you open its mouth, you will find a shekel" (Matt. 17:27 NASB). The fish Peter caught had a coin in its mouth, enough to pay their taxes. Peter had faith to do what Jesus said, and experienced the miracle of retrieving the gold coin from the fish's mouth.

I believe God can do the same for us. His Word wasn't just for the Jews or for the Bible characters we turn into children's stories, but for us, the Gentiles, who are now fellow heirs and partakers of God's promises. He wants us to experience His love and truly understand that He is willing to do exceedingly above all that we dare ask or even think of. We simply need to believe in our hearts that He loves us and wants the best for us, and that He will guide us through His Spirit to fulfill our needs.

When we seek God over what the world gives for our time and effort, we won't regret it. When we assume our positions as daughters of God, He'll ask us what we want. Nothing is too big for God to give those who make Him the focus of their lives; He promises "nations as [presents]" and "continents as [prizes]" (Ps. 2:7–9 MSG).

Once Elton had his Damascus Road experience, he was so hungry for the Word that I began looking for a teaching series to send him while he was overseas. A pastor referred me to a woman who purchased a well-known megapreacher's material in bulk and sold it locally. I began purchasing the CDs and DVDs from her and sending them to Elton, and eventually I became absorbed in the teachings as well.

Several months later Elton came home for a deployment break and wanted to visit the pastor who'd connected me to the woman selling the teaching materials. I reluctantly went with him, unsure why it was so important for Elton to visit her during his two weeks home.

As our conversation with the pastor died down, I mentioned the woman she'd referred me to and how thankful Elton and I were for the things we'd learned. The pastor told me that this woman purchased the CDs and DVDs with the money she needed for special shoes, and that she resold the series below cost to facilitate spreading the Word of God to all who were hungry for it. She sacrificed her own needs to make this teaching series available.

I was touched and suddenly remembered looking at the woman's shoes several weeks before. I had wanted to buy her a new pair but had convinced myself she would be offended by this gesture. After all, it was weird to buy a pair of shoes for someone who was practically a stranger.

When I shared this with the pastor, she looked me in the eye and said, "Baby, that's called being sensitive to the Spirit." She explained that if I could be in tune with the Spirit for shoes, then there was no telling how many more obedience opportunities would come my way.

When I called the woman and told her of my desire to purchase shoes for her, it turned out she had just purchased three pairs a few days earlier. The shoes were such an unusual find that she'd broken down and bought them on her credit card. I offered to reimburse her for all three pairs, suggesting that I could meet her at her home to bring her the money.

Then she told me what the total was. My jaw dropped. I was not expecting her to say $300. I had only $400 in my checking account until payday a few days later, $90 of which was already needed for my daughter's daycare. But this was my first opportunity to give sacrificially, and even though it felt like I had put my foot in my mouth, I was going to follow through.

When I got to her home, I looked at the large house, which was next to a golf course, and I thought, this lady doesn't need my money. I couldn't stop myself from comparing her beautifully decorated home to my partially furnished house; I felt certain that giving to her wasn't adding up. Nonetheless, I knew I had to stay true to my word, even if I had to do so trembling. I left there with a little void inside, wondering if God really had wanted me to give in that capacity.

Two days later I received a letter dated the day after I'd visited the woman's house. It said that my rating from a service-connected disability had increased by 20 percent and that I should expect $1,200 of back pay deposited immediately. Talk about just on time!

The victory I experienced through this obedience opportunity fueled my willingness to continue walking in faith. Now I was eager to operate in this realm and soon had the opportunity to reach yet another level of trust.

In December 2008 I heard a message that would change my life forever. The speaker said that as a child of God I was created for charitable works that required money; my willingness would cause resources to flow through me for God's glory. I was going to be a Kingdom Millionaire—a metaphor for having supernatural abundance in support of the calling in my life. I learned that God promised wealth and abundance to me and that when my motivation was to please God, I would be blessed so I could be a blessing to others. The pathway to this, I understood, was worshipful giving, where I would focus on His greatness and saturate myself in Him. Worship would continue when I gave cheerfully, understanding that He was my sole provider and that I could depend on Him fully.

The message overwhelmed me with the desire to give abundantly. In that moment God became even more real to me, which made me sensitive to His promptings. For the first time in my life, I sowed a significant seed of $1,000. I was in radical faith to be among those financing the advancement of the kingdom of God. I wanted to be the one who funded the missionaries, built the sanctuaries, and provided for God's work around the world. I decided that a tax business was the way to make it all happen. I thought I'd need to be an entrepreneur to bear out that gift of giving, but I had no idea what the process would really entail.

Within two weeks I had applied for a loan and quit my job, opening the doors to my business shortly after tax season began. Then two months later my husband was reassigned to Fort Lewis, and my support system was broken. Everything began falling apart. I realized that the additional expense of his household at Fort Lewis and mine at Fort Hood would make it impossible for me to stay afloat until the business could pay off—not to mention the fact that I didn't have a clue how to run a business.

The tax season was almost over when I got my reality check. In fact, we nearly lost our home! It was time for a change of plans. I figured that if I was a CPA, I could shift my focus from a seasonal tax business and attract year-round clientele. However, I would need one year of work experience under a licensed CPA and about thirty college credits in addition to the accounting credits I already had.

Then I remembered the CPA I'd met months earlier. She worked at an auditing agency, and though I wasn't looking for a job at the time—I was about to be a Kingdom Millionaire!—she'd explained that they usually hired veterans with a bachelor's degree in business- or accounting-related fields. Because I had those qualifications, she'd given me her business card and told me to come back in January when they'd be hiring.

But how could I go there in March when she'd asked me to come back in January? My husband encouraged me not to let my pride get in the way, so I found an old résumé and headed over to the office.

When I arrived, the CPA I'd met before said they had just completed two interviews, but she would see if the panel was willing to interview one more applicant. But when I interviewed with them two days later, it didn't go well at all. Almost every response I offered was twisted into a reason I wouldn't be a good fit for the organization. It felt like such a waste of time. My anxiety began to build as I frantically tried to figure out a plan to bounce back from the situation I'd found myself in.

I was scheduled to attend a women's conference a few weeks later, and before I left I remember thinking, "Okay, God, I'm up a creek with no paddle, tax season is over, I have no job, my husband is stationed at Lewis, my house won't sell, I don't want to leave my church, You dropped this hot message in my bosom, and every open door seemed to confirm I was headed in the right direction, but now I'm in some serious debt from setting up shop—what's up?" That's when I realized that I was running with God's vision but hadn't stopped long enough to ensure I was still on the right path. I looked around and didn't sense Him by my side. For the first time in maybe months I asked, "God, please show me what to do."

I heard Him clearly say, "Business checking account."

I knew I had about $5,000 left (and then I perish), and $1,000 already had checks written against it. I said, "You've got to be kidding me; You want me to sow the $4,000?" I couldn't even tell my husband, it sounded so crazy.

At the women's conference, the preacher whose words had first stirred me to begin giving months prior spoke prophetically, saying that one hundred women would sow $1,000 for the ministry. I was superexcited—I was willing to give up $1,000, but not the full amount in my business checking account—so I sowed the $1,000. I thought it was my ram in the bush, like in the story of Abraham. Abraham was ready to sacrifice his son, Isaac, when a ram appeared at the last minute for him to sacrifice instead; he'd passed the test by showing his willingness to obey God at any cost (Gen. 22). Maybe I didn't have to sacrifice the whole $4,000 after all! I was elated; in that moment I felt like God was on my side once again, and I was prepared to follow His instructions step by step. I was in an atmosphere of faith and ready to download from heaven the words of wisdom God would share through the speakers for my specific situation.

The next evening another preacher shared the story of a woman who was about to lose her home and her car. This woman had asked the speaker for money to eat, and she gave her a check instead of cash. The woman assumed the check was only for a small amount and never even looked at it or deposited it. As expected, she lost her home and her car, which caused her to question God. One day she finally decided to deposit the check and realized that it would have been enough to cover her mortgage and car payments. The preacher reminded us that when we have faith in God, we need to "check our checks" and be in anticipation of God coming through for us on time. That night I checked all the mail I could— including my voicemail and email—just in case I'd missed a call for the job or some other miracle. Nothing!

The following morning a different preacher spoke about how she'd given a significant seed of $3,000 the year before, the last in her business checking account, and she was reaping it that year even as the conference was going on. I could hardly believe what I was hearing. I'd heard Him say, "Business checking account," and now this woman was talking about the last in her own business checking account—and it was exactly what I had left after giving $1,000 during the first appeal. I was sold.

I called my husband and told him everything.

"Go for it!" he said.

Boom, we're out there—out of the boat—ready to walk on water, like Peter did in faith. That Friday night I sowed the money, trembling. At the end of the service, one of the conference hosts shared a verse (Genesis 26:12) that promised a hundredfold return to those who sowed sacrificially in obedience to God's promptings. She also prophesied that we could expect the return by the same time the following year, though she explained that a hundredfold didn't necessarily mean one hundred times the amount, but God's best.

The very weekend I gave that seed at the women's conference, I got a call for the job I'm currently in. They'd left a phone message on the Thursday, but I hadn't seen it, even though I'd checked my voicemail. Being offered that job was a miracle, and I considered it the beginning of the manifestation of all that was prophesied during the conference. The verse sustained me through the entire year, including a near foreclosure on our house, a failed business, and confessions that should have derailed our marriage. The following year I showed up at the conference with even greater expectation. This weekend was God's last chance to bring His word to pass in my life. I was high!

I attended every session, believing that this moment could be the one where something revelatory would astound me. But although each speaker was great, nothing seemed personalized for me yet. I didn't waver in my expectation. On the final night of the conference, I put on my Sunday best—God was about to do it, and I wanted to look the part. I don't know what I was expecting exactly, but I was sure it was going to be big. I yearned for the manifested power of God and for Him to do something that only He could do. Even when the conference ended, I still hoped that something tangible would take place in my life. During my three-hour drive home I stayed dressed up the whole way because I figured God could meet me at a gas station on the way and still do it big. It was the last hour; God was cutting it close, but something was bound to happen.

I made it home and got into bed, crushed. I had believed that my expectation was God's invitation to move miraculously in my life. I wondered what I had done wrong, what I had missed, why He hadn't shown me His glory. I felt like heaven and hell were both laughing at my elementary attempt at being in faith.

During praise and worship the following Sunday, I was singing on stage when the presence of God filled the sanctuary. I asked Him, "What happened? You said by this time next year, a hundredfold!"

He said, "Baby, what you got was the anointing!" I didn't even know what He meant. I speculated and sensed my sphere of influence would increase, but that was the extent of it. Still, since I could hear His voice, I felt hope.

The words *anointing* and *favor* are thrown around in Christian circles all the time; I'm so grateful to our guest speaker that Sunday for breaking them down. She explained that anointing oil was originally put on sheep to protect and identify them and to keep bugs from laying eggs in their ears. The slip of the oil would prevent the eggs from nestling and hatching there and causing the sheep to stray from the invasive feeling of foreign beings. Figuratively, receiving God's anointing meant that He would place a hedge of protection around me because I was His child. Others would know that I belonged to Him because of the distinct fragrance that He would use. In addition, His anointing would prevent negative chatter and harmful self-talk from taking root and driving me away from His purpose for my life.

The speaker's message gave me a deeper appreciation for God telling me personally that I'd received the anointing. I realized I could value the lessons I'd learned through my trials and understand that hardship was never meant to make me bitter, but to bring out the best in me.

Because I was simply looking for a fat paycheck, I felt like my prayers weren't answered. In fact, what looked like a bad year was a setup for my greater good. When I adjusted my perspective I realized that what I got was better than cash. It was God's provision—His hand on my life and His guidance, wisdom, protection, and innovation.

Sometimes I miss God because I'm looking for

Him in the wrong places. But praise God, at least I'm looking! I was so grateful that He sealed this revelation in my heart. It seemed like nothing had happened, when in fact so much had.

While on my new job, I had become friends with one of my coworkers, who was a Christian too. We shared an office and had some great conversations, but one particularly stood out for me: her awesome testimony of finishing her master's degree and sitting for the CPA exam before turning thirty. What was really amazing was that she did the majority of this as a single mother of four.

As I listened to her story, I noticed the Scriptures pinned to her corkboard—the parable of the ten talents (Matt. 25:14-30). I don't think I had ever read it in that version before, and the words "wicked and lazy and idle servant" jumped out at me.

The parable is about a master who gave three of his servants different measures of talents or abilities. To one he gave five; to another, two; and to a third servant he gave just one talent. The first two invested and multiplied their talents to ten and four, respectively. The servant who was given one talent buried it because he thought his master was a harsh and hard man who reaped where he didn't sow. The master called him a wicked, lazy, and idle servant and took his talent away and gave it to the one who now had ten.

This parable was always a favorite of mine, but I had never focused on how the servant was viewed by the master for not maximizing his opportunities. Here I was, admiring this woman for achieving her goals at such a young age, when I too had the same opportunity—with fewer responsibilities.

I called my husband to share my revelation, and as we spoke he actually made a U-turn, driving to the local college to begin the enrollment process immediately. It was something I had encouraged him to do for many years, but nothing I said before had convinced him to get started. That day my coworker's story and the Scriptures on her corkboard inspired us both. I stopped procrastinating and finally enrolled in the master's program at the local college—something I needed to do to sit for the CPA exam, but that I'd kept putting off because my husband was gone.

In the meantime, Elton was able to maximize our time apart to take full-time courses even though he was still working full-time. A year later he learned of a degree completion program the military offered, one that would allow him to attend college full-time and still get paid his salary. The courses he'd taken during that year apart were exactly what he needed to qualify for the program.

Some of my story may seem a little shallow—a house, a job, an assignment—in comparison with the life-threatening ordeals that people face every day. However, faith is like a muscle; we have to exercise it, and practicing faith on those ordinary things means our muscles will be ready to flex when it's time to conquer mountains. God will fight our battles, but we have to show up. We have to be prepared to engage in the fight of faith.

God's got our backs when we jump ahead, fall flat on our faces, and misinterpret His guidance, and even when others are taking advantage of us. The condition of our hearts is what matters, not our circumstances. I've learned that the kingdom of God is comparable to the farming process. Although the farmer plants the seed, he doesn't know how the seeds sprout and grow—but when the crop is ready he wastes no time harvesting it (Mark 4:26–29). Often I'm more concerned with the how than with trusting the process. Other times, I procrastinate with following through in obedience because I can't fathom how my actions would produce a harvest. I know now that I have to let God reveal the method over time while I enjoy the journey.

I truly believe that our victories are tied to our willingness to give, our willingness to trust God at His word. Malachi 3:10 shows that when we give tithes and offerings, we're taking care of God's house. When we take care of God's house, He opens the windows of heaven and pours out a blessing so vast that there's not room enough for us to receive it. These are just a few of my stories that I associate with giving, but there are so many more, and the details are mind-blowing.

My dream of being a successful entrepreneur hasn't died. The purpose for my success is still alive. Anything worth having is worth fighting for. Besides pouring out blessings, God promises to rebuke the devourer for our sake. I've made mistakes, and many circumstances have come my way that could have taken me out of the race, but God is faithful to His word and put a stop to it. He can do the same for all of us.

Childlike Faith Exercises

I encourage you to tithe and give consistently. It pays to obey God, and giving positions you to do more. If you've never done this before, now is the perfect time to get started. God wants you to test Him in this promise. He is so ready to prove to you that this strategy works. Victory is yours!

Determine your income from all sources and commit to give a tithe (10 percent) to your church.

Purpose in your heart an offering amount above your tithe to give to your church regularly.

If you struggle with giving, identify what's holding you back and pray for those hindrances to be removed.

If you don't have a church, connect with a faith community where you can learn more about God, the gift of Jesus, the power of the Holy Spirit, and everything God has to say about financial increase.

Prayer

Dear God,

I praise You for who You are and all that You've done for me. Thank You for revealing how giving enables me to receive of Your financial abundance. I trust that Your instructions are for my good, so that I can experience heaven here on earth. Thank You, Father, for Your divine wisdom, guidance, and provision. I cast my cares on You! I set my attention and focus on You, Lord. Give me the courage to serve You continually and to recognize money as a tool and not my source. You are my provider, and You have my heart and my treasures. In Jesus' name. Amen.

Chapter 6

Sensitive to the Spirit

A little cash is always nice, but God leaves us in utter awe when He uses us to inspire the life of another through our sensitivity to the Spirit. God's ways go far beyond material needs and support. Every day we're faced with life-and-death situations (Deut. 30:15–20), but because our everyday choices never look critical, we're blinded into thinking we can make these decisions lightly. Even the seemingly insignificant choices are important because each positions us closer or further from the will of God.

I remember going to the commissary to pick up groceries with my husband one sunny afternoon. You know how we always hear not to go grocery shopping when we're hungry, because we'll probably buy a lot more junk food? This time we really should have eaten before we went. By the time we were done shopping, our cart was full of unhealthy, high-calorie packaged goods, and I knew we had gone over the budget.

I cringed as the cashier rang us up. Even though it probably made sense to put some of those items back, the register was not where I wanted to make that decision. "Paper or plastic?" the bagger asked me, and I realized that I'd have to spend even more to cover her tip—baggers at military commissaries work for tips only. I was at a crossroads, though in the moment it didn't seem too critical. To tip or not to tip? Don't judge me, I thought—I'm going to bag my own groceries!

The Holy Spirit is always right there with us, and He gently nudges us even during what seem like unimportant moments. I truly felt Him that afternoon, and I rejected the thought to avoid tipping. "Paper," I told her with a smile.

As we chatted on our way out of the commissary, I asked my husband for the tip money and decided to give the woman a church invitation card too. What happened next blew me away.

Elton told her that she could come to church

dressed as she was. He was simply trying to make her feel welcome, but she seemed upset, telling us that the church she used to go to was really strict—she couldn't show up at our church any old kind of way.

It's crazy how even when we're trying to do good, our sinful nature wants to throw us two steps backward. I was immediately offended; I felt that she had already judged me, assuming that our church didn't honor God if it wasn't strict about dress. In that split second the invitation could have ended right there.

I wanted to snatch the card out of her hands and tell her to go back to her stuffy church. I was pleasantly surprised that what came out of my mouth instead was an explanation about how God was concerned more with the condition of her heart than her clothes; that was the only reason we'd even mentioned it. It broke the ice and she broke down, sharing that just the day before, she had wanted to end her life. Getting the invitation to church was her assurance that God still loved her.

I was so touched by the experience that I wrote a song about it the next morning.

Ran into a lady at the commissary
She works for a living bagging my groceries
What should I tip her today?
Spent $230 (higher than usual)
I'll grab my own stuff; won't have enough
Don't feel like tipping today.
Somehow I knew God wanted more
Use me, Lord, once more
Won't pass this chance, this is my test
He wants to bless once more
We walk out together, ask hubby to tip her
Reach for my purse, pass an invite to church
That's how God wants it to go
Strike up conversation, wind up on redemption
God has a plan for a beautiful end
That's what God wants her to know
The last two years were rough
She questioned God, When is enough
She tried to end her life one day
She was so hurt, she hates the pain
Holy Spirit kicked right in
It's not God's fault, you know
He wants to change your life today
His Son died just for you

Use me, Lord, I know that You wanna do more
Use me, Lord, to reach the hurt and lost
I wanna be the vessel that You choose to use
I'll listen for Your guidance
I'll do what You want me to

Even though the song doesn't go into so much detail, the woman cried, hugged me, and shared her deepest pain with me, then apologized for doing so to a complete stranger. She walked away shaking her head and looking at the church invitation again and again as my husband and I just watched her in awe.

That encounter left us breathless. We didn't normally even shop at the commissary, but God orchestrated the smallest details so we could be where we were needed that day. We sensed His presence in that parking lot and felt maybe even more blessed than she did.

Having lived in Texas for so long, I liked big things—big opportunities and big results—but on that day I realized that big opportunities may come in unlikely places. The results may not be monetary, but God knows just how to fulfill us with purpose. Sometimes the simplest decision—to tip or not to tip, to be offended or not to be offended—is the only difference between being used by God or giving God a bad name.

Childlike faith is handing an invitation to church to a complete stranger, such a simple act with no obvious promise of grand results, and experiencing the grown-up miracle of God reaching someone through our actions. When we allow the Holy Spirit to lead us, we are given the right things to say or do at just the right moment in just the right place (Rom. 8:12–39). Being led by the Spirit is a life of adventure, where childlike faith in obeying a prompting of the Spirit unfolds into a miraculous manifestation of our deepest desires.

John 16:12–15 teaches that the Spirit of Truth is there to guide us into all the truth there is, and that He will make sense out of what will happen. Over the years, I've enjoyed opportunities to be sensitive to the Spirit in greater measure, and I continue to be rewarded immensely. Sometimes the rewards are immediate; sometimes not. However, with each opportunity to follow the Spirit's lead, my faith and my trust in His voice grow exponentially.

Shortly after we joined our new church, our pastor

had an altar call for salvation—including an appeal for anyone wanting to speak in tongues. I shot my husband a look. When Elton had first gotten saved, he had mentioned the benefits of speaking in tongues, telling me he wanted the full power made available to him through Jesus Christ. Personally, I wasn't interested—too spooky, I thought—but now I nudged him and pointed out that this was his opportunity to find out if he could speak in this heavenly language. Elton was sensitive to the Spirit; he went to the altar without hesitation.

When he left the prayer room later, he had a glow about him—and a swagger that told me he had positively spoken in tongues. To my surprise, I felt like I had missed out. The benefits of speaking in tongues seemed suddenly less farfetched. That night when we got home, we got on our faces and prayed for me to also receive the gift of this heavenly language. Slowly but surely my mouth got its own motor, and everything that was pent up inside me flowed out of my lips.

Speaking in tongues is a spiritual endeavor that requires believing. My husband believed when he went into that prayer room. He was of one accord with the woman who prayed with him, and was filled with the Holy Spirit—whose power manifested itself through the gift of tongues. I later believed what my husband told me, and my faith was stirred to receive the same gift. It's only by the Spirit that we could both desire and receive the same.

So what exactly does it mean to speak in tongues? Put simply, it is speaking in an unknown language as inspired by the Holy Spirit. Acts 2 describes how this happened on the day of Pentecost, when those gathered in the room were filled with the Holy Spirit and began speaking in other tongues. The crowds were amazed because they heard about the wonderful works of God—each in their own language.

Imagine being able to instantly speak in another language for the sake of facilitating communication and preaching the gospel of Jesus Christ! Acts 10 describes how Gentiles also received the gift of the Holy Spirit and began to speak in tongues. This is important because here we find the Scripture that says God is no respecter of race, nationality, or background: "But in every nation he that feareth him, and worketh righteousness, is accepted with him" (Acts 10:35). Thankfully, being accepted by God isn't limited to a select few. The Holy Spirit and the gift of tongues are available to all.

Speaking another language is amazing. But even more powerful is the gift He gives us today: the ability to speak to God in an inspired language in such a way that we're communicating God's intent right back at Him, compelling Him to execute the thoughts and plans He's had for us since the beginning of time. Whoa! Read that sentence again.

As believers, it's our responsibility to be aware of God's promises, lay hold of our inheritance through Jesus Christ, and understand the purpose of our inheritance. Jesus promised that God would send us another friend, the Spirit of Truth, a Comforter, Counselor, Helper, Intercessor, Advocate, Strengthener—the Holy Spirit, who would teach us all things and remind us of everything that Jesus shared. The Holy Spirit exercises all of these roles for us constantly. He is a gift from God, just as Jesus was a gift.

1 Corinthians 12 explains that each of us is given a manifestation of the Spirit for the benefit of all; the Holy Spirit decides who gets these gifts and when the gifts will manifest.

The variety is wonderful:

wise counsel

clear understanding

simple trust

healing the sick

miraculous acts

proclamation

distinguishing between spirits

tongues

interpretation of tongues"

(1 Corinthians 12:27–31 MSG).

Later, in 1 Corinthians 14, Paul encourages us to desire and cultivate the spiritual gifts. One such gift is prophecy, or the ability to interpret God's divine will through inspired preaching and teaching. This gift is especially valued because it helps to build up others and encourage them as they grow in their walk with God.

In that same chapter Paul makes a case for the perhaps less-coveted gift of speaking in tongues. Specifically, he states that those who speak in an unknown tongue speak not to people but to God, because in the Holy Spirit they utter secret truths and hidden things not obvious to the understanding. Speaking in tongues builds us up and facilitates self-improvement.

Paul encourages the church to focus on prophesying when in a corporate setting, so that everyone can benefit from what is being said. But that doesn't mean the gift of tongues should be overlooked. In fact, Paul still expresses his desire for all to speak in unknown tongues and concludes that we should not forbid or hinder the use of this gift. I liken it to loving our neighbor as we love ourselves. If we neglect to love ourselves, how can our expression of love to others be any better? If we neglect to build ourselves up through speaking in tongues, how will we be able to prophesy for the benefit of others?

The faith process can be even more rewarding when strategically coupled with declarations that line up with what God has already planned for us. I truly believe that being able to speak in tongues to God is one of the most powerful gifts a Christian has at her disposal, and one she shouldn't do without. Earlier I shared how a coworker's statement about God spoiling baby Christians inspired me to milk it through great expectation of my inheritance in Christ. For me, milking it was having my laundry list of desires constantly before God. In this newfound life and adventure, I had dreams that only God could orchestrate, and I wanted to make the most of my Christian experience. Speaking in tongues helped me do just that.

Although I was a baby Christian, I was immediately pregnant with expectation of what God would do for me, in me, and through me. As with physical pregnancy, most of the time I was giddy with anticipation, but there were days when the waiting was unbearable. Figuratively, I didn't know if I was having a boy or a girl, or maybe even twins. Would my baby come early or way past its due date? In fact, when was the due date in the first place? When God wants to birth from us a spiritual thing, there will be times when we're just tired of being pregnant, and we struggle with the unknown.

I remember feeling this way toward the end of my pregnancy with my daughter. I just wanted her to come already, but to have her own birthday—three of my sisters and my mother and grandmother all had birthdays within a few days of my daughter's due date.

In the scheme of things, I could have spent more time praying for her to be healthy and whole. Instead I was praying for her birthday to be on a different day. In fact, I was so desperate to have her that I decided to eat okra, lots of it, because I'd read that it might make me go into labor quickly. Whew! She was born on December 24, a day all her own—and I'm sure the okra had nothing to do with it.

Being desperate meant that I took unnecessary measures to help the pregnancy along instead of focusing on what really mattered. The same can happen as we wait in expectation for the manifestation of God's promises.

Often we're in the middle of birthing the most amazing victory ever, yet find we don't know what or how to pray. We have access to the most Supreme Being, God Himself, but we ask for trivial things. However, when we pray in tongues we are praying the most strategic and accurate prayer we can use to unleash heaven on our behalf. Speaking in heavenly tongues gives us insider knowledge of what God is willing to do and an advocate to ensure His will is executed. When we don't know how or what to pray, the Holy Spirit "goes to meet our supplication and pleads in our behalf with unspeakable yearnings and groanings too deep for utterance" (Rom. 8:26 AB). It is through the Holy Spirit that we can utter secret truths and hidden mysteries not obvious to our own understanding.

Once we receive the gift of the Holy Spirit, we are empowered to speak directly to God in a way no one else can comprehend. Whether the infilling of the Holy Spirit occurs in a large or a more intimate setting, the key is to believe enough to open our mouths and know that the Holy Spirit will speak through us. It may be awkward at first or even sound like gibberish, but as we surrender He'll take over and intercede on our behalf. It takes childlike faith to experience this very grown-up miracle of speaking to God strategically and accurately.

A wise Christian doesn't try to figure it out on her own but realizes that God is a god of order and principle. Recognizing, adopting, and implementing the systems that God has in place to ensure our success shows that we trust God and His ways over our own. We will exhibit the fruit of the Spirit—love, joy, peace, longsuffering, gentleness, goodness, and yes, faith—and with these we will be empowered to exercise the power of the Holy Spirit to speak in tongues. Then, as we build ourselves up by praying in the Holy Spirit, we will remain at the center of God's love and mercy.

Childlike Faith Exercises

Purpose in your heart to obey the next prompting of the Holy Spirit. Pray that an opportunity will come quickly so you can seal it in your heart right away.

Identify one Scripture that gives you hope and one personal experience that shows this Scripture operating in your life. The time will come to share that Scripture and story with someone. Wait for that opportunity in faith.

If you already speak in tongues, do it consistently this week and pay attention to the events taking place in your life. Be prepared to marvel.

If you don't know how to speak in tongues, find a church that believes in this gift. Connect with helpers there who can pray with you to receive it.

Prayer

Dear God,

Thank You, Father God, for Your mere existence and for Your desire to reward me for seeking You! Thank You for Your Son, Jesus, who died for my freedom. Thank You for Your Holy Spirit, who confirms who I am and that I belong to You. I thank You for the good times ahead and welcome You as my guide into all that You have for me and all that You will do through me. Enlarge me in my hour of waiting and let my joy be full as I anticipate Your goodness. Thank You, Lord, for provision throughout this journey. Thank You for Your heart toward me. Give me Your heart for others. I'm so ready for this adventure of childlike faith through Your Spirit. Give me my marching orders and be glorified in all I do. Place a hedge of protection around me as I dive headlong into Your will for my life. I give You all the glory and honor. In Jesus' name. Amen.

Chapter 7

It's Never Too Late to Follow Your Dreams

I've been singing ever since I was a little girl. I can remember the times I would sing and dance in front of the mirror, a hairbrush microphone in my hand, giving my imaginary audience my most dazzling smile. I still have vivid memories of wearing a costume to represent Haiti in my school's rendition of "It's a Small World (After All)." I was maybe five years old, but it was exhilarating. I wanted to be a star.

As I grew older, I began buying soundtrack cassettes with the vocals on one side and the instrumentals on the other. Every week I'd learn a few new songs to sing at church the following weekend. Later, when I stopped attending church, you could find me at a club on karaoke night, singing my heart out. It didn't matter where I was—singing was in me. I relished every opportunity.

I was flying home to Texas when songwriting surfaced in my adult life. I still remember the song I was listening to, and the way a different set of lyrics and a complementary melody formed above the music blaring through my headphones. It was such a pleasant surprise that even though I wrote the lyrics down, I kept thinking they must be from some other song I had subconsciously remembered from a long time before. In fact, I searched more than once just to be sure it was my original song. It was. That day in June 2009, I discovered that I was a songwriter.

This happened shortly after I gave sacrificially at the women's conference mentioned earlier. Suddenly, inspiration was everywhere. I would write new songs inspired by a series of messages my pastor preached, or by extraordinary everyday encounters (like the woman bagging my groceries at the commissary). Sometimes my daughter and I responded to each other in song. She had nuggets of wisdom beyond her years, but it would drive her brother and dad crazy that we'd sing at the top of our lungs until we burst into laughter.

The months that followed were a whirlwind of

songwriting experiences that left me in awe because I was sure God was breathing these songs over me. Each song I wrote encouraged me in an awesome way, and my fellow musicians were supportive of my dream to bring the music and lyrics to life. I was ready for the world to enjoy them now.

The first song I chose to work on was inspired by a sermon that fueled my passion to go the distance in pursuing my dreams. I couldn't wait to share it. But maybe I should have.

Although the song was still in rough form, I hoped the person who heard it first could offer me feedback on the lyrics. Perhaps I should have clarified what I wanted; instead what I received was his opinion that the song sounded as bad as he did. This person couldn't carry a tune—he knew it, too—and I was crushed. Even when I tried to dismiss his words or find ways to explain what he'd said, I struggled to shake the effect they were having on me.

I became self-conscious and began not only to doubt my ability to sing but even to deny the gift of songwriting. It seemed like everything I did related to music was met with opposition and negativity. The desire to share my creativity vanished; it would come back in spurts, only to be extinguished again. I was caught in a vicious circle of dreaming and quitting and wishing I didn't have the desire or the gift in the first place.

In one of my dreaming spells, I cried out to God and asked for direction. To my surprise, I clearly heard Him give me the title of a book. It wasn't a book I had heard of before; in fact, I only realized it was a book title when I decided to look up the phrase He gave me. I began to read it immediately.

In the third chapter, the author tells how he wrote some songs and asked for feedback from someone whose opinion he valued. His friend told him the songs sounded terrible—but then several months later, that same friend asked about the songs and wondered when he would record them. The author had thought his friend hated the songs, but it turned out to be the opposite; it was the quality of the recording that was poor. That's a big difference.

I had already received clarification from my own critic, who'd explained that he was referring to the quality of the recording too. However, I had taken it so personally that I'd ignored his words, assuming he was just trying to do some damage control. Reading the author's story helped me see things from a different perspective. It was the beginning of the process of getting me unstuck and into a place where I could let go of my insecurities.

Imagine that! Isn't it just like God to send us a timely word to help us get over our hurt? With the past behind me, I could dream again and take practical steps to follow those dreams.

Once I started dreaming again, I learned that being filled with the Spirit made way for speaking in psalms, hymns, and spiritual songs. Singing in my heart to the Lord was a direct result of being in a relationship with Him (Eph. 5:19). I finally understood that I didn't need anyone's approval; the mere fact that music was forming in my heart was proof that I had God's approval already. I was in a relationship with the very person who could make all my dreams come true. He had given me a gift that I thought could surely bring fame and fortune.

Oftentimes we ask God for help in only one aspect of our dreams. We don't really surrender our entire dream to Him because we don't want or know how to relinquish control. We say that we've made Jesus Lord over our lives, but we haven't handed over the reins. What we actually want is for God to be our most faithful employee instead of the CEO of our lives.

Not surprisingly, many of our prayers seem to go unanswered because the tasks we give this faithful employee don't line up with our deepest desires—which He knows so well. Some of the things we want would only temporarily satisfy us, and soon we'd discover we wanted our faithful employee to do something different. James 4:2–3 says that we have not because we ask not, and when we do, we ask amiss, i.e., with selfish motives. The good thing about God is that He is more than a faithful employee; He's a visionary, a CEO, and His plan is to wow us beyond what we could expect. He assures us in Jeremiah 29:11 that the thoughts He has toward us are "of peace and not evil, to give us an expected end."

I was expecting my music to become wildly popular and make me a ton of money. Imagine my confusion when I sensed God wanted me to attend a small group Bible study at my church on a day that conflicted with our scheduled choir rehearsals. Certainly, I thought, this was not of God; the enemy was trying to trick me into giving up my role in the choir! I was born to sing. Couldn't I read the study book on my own time and still do what I loved? Better yet, perhaps my faithful employee could encourage the pastors to put these events on different days so that I could do both.

I was torn. But with a study theme like *What Happens When Women Say Yes to God*, what was I to do? I reluctantly quit the choir and showed up to the first study session with the book in my hand and tears in my eyes. But the longer I attended the Bible study, the more I realized it was meant to be. I learned so much during that time and connected with precious women who in their own way were saying yes to God. I still have the study book and flip through it occasionally.

When I was looking through it while writing this book, I finally grasped just how much God had answered my prayers during that season of my life. During the study I'd learned that being a woman who says yes to God means making the choice to trust Him even when we can't understand why He requires some of the things He does. It also means that once we've said yes to Him, we refuse to turn back—even when things get hard. Boy, do I wish I'd remembered that part along the way!

At the end of the first chapter, I had written a personal prayer of commitment for my new adventure with God:

Father God,

For nearly a year now I've felt like You wanted me to be available for other areas of ministry. I have struggled with this and even questioned whether my own flesh prompted the desire to be elsewhere. I have fought it and yielded reluctantly, even wondering if I were making a mistake—afraid of missing out on being where You intend to bless me. Well, Lord, this prayer is to say that I surrender it all to You, that I trust You, and that even if I didn't hear You correctly, I trust You will restore the years that the cankerworm has stolen or may be stealing right now. I trust that Your Word says that all things work together for my good. I thank You that You are all I need and that my trust should be solely in You. Everything I need is in Your hands. I thank You that my choices have grown from being between right and wrong, good and better, to between better and best. I surrender my life to You, and I know You gave me these desires and

> *this personality, and that You would never require me to do something contrary to who You created me to be. Thank You, God, that the thoughts You have of me are of good and not evil, and that You will get me to my expected end. You are amazing. I love You, God, for all You are and all You do. In Jesus' name. Amen.*

Even as I read those words, I choked up. I remember how vulnerable I was the day I wrote them, and how afraid I was of making a choice that I thought could delay or derail my destiny. I could see how scripted my prayer was and how many of my true fears were omitted—as if God couldn't search my heart and know my deepest desires and wildest dreams. Jeremiah 17 tells us that God searches all hearts and examines our secret motives to reward us accordingly. If there's anyone we should practice keeping it real with, it's our Father in heaven.

Even though I'd surrendered my dreams to God, soon after the study ended I found myself trying to take control again. I didn't know what to do with that empty space. What I should have been doing was resting in the Lord and waiting patiently for Him (Ps.

37:7). Instead I tried going back to choir and got involved in other areas at church. I was unsettled and unfulfilled.

Although my dream to be a successful singer-songwriter hadn't died, I knew that I needed to remove the pressure to have it fulfilled through my church. I wanted God to finish the work He'd begun in me. My willingness to put this dream on the back burner, if only for a while, was a necessary sacrifice to nurture and operate in the other talents He had given me. One day, as I mindlessly scrolled through my social media feed, I cried out to God that there had to be more. I needed Him to show me what to do.

The next thing that caught my attention was an advertisement for a course on how to open an online store. That was all it took; I signed up, and while I waited for it to start I received an invitation from the same company to attend a different teleseminar a few days later. For months I took course after course, gradually realizing that my connection to the marketing consultant conducting the course was divinely orchestrated.

When you make God the CEO of your life, He shares insights on the experiences you didn't quite understand and gives you an appreciation for all you've been through on your journey. Discovering that God is in the details has an amazing way of enticing you to find and trust Him in all that you do.

Several months after I said yes to God, I'd had a business idea. It was so simple that I somewhat took it for granted, though I continued to pray for God to show me what to do. I was afraid to begin. My idea to start a tax business had been a disaster; I had moved out swiftly and almost lost our home. I was leery of putting my family through one of my ideas again.

But when the marketing consultant introduced her vision during the teleseminar, I was blown away by the similarities to the business idea that was still in the back of my mind—and by the fact that she had the complete blueprint to make it happen. With every course I took, God used her to show me what to do.

Often plans fail for lack of counsel and advisers (Prov. 15:22), but when you commit to the Lord whatever you do, your plans will succeed (Prov. 16:3). God knew what I needed and allowed our paths to cross at a defining intersection in my life (Prov. 16:9).

Even though the connection seemed divine, I continued to seek clarity. Have you ever wished that

God would just write on the wall exactly what you should be doing? I've wanted that type of clarity on many occasions, yet never wanted it enough to wait patiently for a response.

But when I'm still long enough, God grants my desires and shares exactly what He wants me to focus on. About a week after I started the online store course, He did it through my dreams. I dreamed that I was in a busy market square in a foreign country. When I try to picture my dream now, the image reminds me of when I was stationed in Saudi Arabia for a short deployment and had the opportunity to shop in dimly lit alleyways for unique trinkets and gold. In both scenes vendors lined either side of the street, but in the dream their faces and products were a blur.

In my dream, I stopped to look at some leather journals sold by a jolly, plump gentleman with silver hair. That is, somehow I knew I was looking at leather journals, but I didn't really have a visual—the products were a blur, remember? The man seemed so kind, and our banter was pleasant as we negotiated the price of the journals. I was glad to be doing business with this fellow.

As we discussed the transaction, a passerby interrupted to ask me a question. I was happy to oblige. In fact, I was in such a good mood that I wanted to take the time to write out my answer. I grabbed a hot pink sticky pad and a pen, both of which appeared out of thin air on the jolly vendor's table.

As I began to write, the vendor playfully pushed the pen out of my hand. I picked up the pen to begin writing again, and he pushed it away once more. Undeterred, I picked up the pen a third time, with every intention of writing what I wanted to give the passerby who'd requested help. This time the vendor grabbed a wooden bat and violently swung it at me as if to stop me from ever trying again.

Since I was dreaming, I suddenly became like a superhero and stopped the bat midswing with my bare hands. In one movement I took possession of the bat and started to beat the jolly fellow, who went from looking plump and pleasant to slick and leathery. His silver locks shriveled up and his blurry features were suddenly clearly defined. He was strong and muscular and evil.

Even though I had the bat and was beating the

daylights out of him with all the strength I could muster, he stood his ground and threw his head back and laughed like evil characters do in comic strips. I was getting tired, and he could see it. He turned and walked away in mockery of my weakness.

Being cocky doesn't pay off, and dismissing this superhero was the wrong move. He should never have discounted me. He should never have turned his back. I made one final blow to the back of his head, and the tables were reversed. He folded like the crease on my favorite page of a book, then crumpled. Finally the life drained out of him like ink from a cheap pen. Dude, I was just trying to write a sticky note to help somebody! Did it have to come to this? I woke from my dream wondering if the passerby with the question ever got what he needed.

Sometimes the enemy only rears his ugly head when we're up to something significant. So long as we're shooting the breeze with him, preoccupied with things outside our purpose, we don't pose a threat. But the minute we take even the smallest step in the direction of our calling, he'll attempt to hinder us. If he succeeds in his first attempt, we may never know just how ugly he is and how powerful we are. When we put in a serious effort to accomplish what we are destined to do, we will surely see him show his true identity—and that's when we will realize we have what it takes.

Greater is He that is in us! We have the power to stop the enemy midstride and do what we are meant to do, be who we are meant to be, have what we are meant to have. We may get weary in working God's plan, but we can outlast the enemy.

The key is to be observant. Where is he trying to stop us? That's most likely where we need to be. It's also important not to discount the small desires to take action, since purpose lies within. It may start with a sticky note but could end up a book. This dream may have taken seconds—far less time than it took to journal it—but in that moment God made it crystal clear. Bottom line for me: focus on writing.

Though I had always known that I would write a book, I'd never considered it a dream to pursue. I suppose I'd thought it would be something I'd do once I experienced success in some other endeavor, like my music. I was dumbfounded that I hadn't previously recognized the obvious calling to write.

Not only did God provide clarity, He already had

helped me find the marketing consultant, who provided training for this dream too—including a teleseminar on becoming a freelance writer. Then during the online store course, she announced that she was writing a book, and in one session she decided to introduce attendees to her publisher. I was excited because I understood that God knew my goals and dreams ahead of time and was already orchestrating things behind the scenes.

I had written about 17,000 words before I found the courage to contact her publisher and take the next step. As I researched their site, I found that they had published several of my latest reads, including the journal to complement the book *What Happens When Women Say Yes to God*. Wow! What a full-circle moment that was for me. My faith was stirred. The possibilities were reeling in my head.

Moments like these fascinate me. God is so meticulous and weaves the lives of others into ours at the precise moment we need them to cause a breakthrough. I spoke to a representative of the publisher, and by the time the conversation was over, I had renewed purpose and accountability. When I sat down to write, the words flowed a little more freely now that I knew others were waiting for my manuscript, ready to spring into action on my behalf.

God wants us to trust Him with our wildest dreams. He wants us to pour out our deepest desires before Him. But God wants to give us a dream that is bigger than any we've ever imagined, and He wants to fulfill desires we can't even articulate. It doesn't matter if we've tried before or if we feel like we're too old or too young to pursue what's in our hearts. God will get us to our expected end.

Childlike Faith Exercises

Make a list of the childhood dreams where you envisioned yourself fulfilling your deepest desires.

Sometimes our dreams evolve over time. Make a list of your present dreams.

Evaluate your present dreams and your childhood dreams against the Word of God to ensure you have identified your deepest desires. Write down the dreams that align with your deepest desires.

Explore the internal factors hindering you from pursuing your God-given dreams. Identify Scriptures that address these factors, like 2 Timothy 1:7 ("For

God has not given us the spirit of fear; but of power, and of love, and of a sound mind").

Write down the external factors you've perceived as hindrances to your dreams. Are your present dreams minimized by naysayers? What else is holding you back? Identify Scriptures showing that these have no power over you. For example, look at Romans 8:31 ("If God be for us, who can be against us?") or Psalm 23:4 ("Yea, though I walk through the valley of the shadow of death, I will fear no evil: for thou art with me; thy rod and thy staff they comfort me").

Rest assured and know that since God is a partner in your labor, all things work together for your good. You are called according to His design and purpose. Take action on a goal or dream and acknowledge God as your partner. He loves you (Rom. 8:28)!

Prayer

Dear God,

I praise You, glorify You, and magnify Your name. You're amazing, and I call Your will into this world and specifically into my life. You know what I need. I thank You for Your provision. Forgive me, Father, for taking things into my own hands and not waiting patiently for Your lead. I release all bitterness and resentment toward the people I expected to play an active role in the fulfillment of my dreams. I place my dreams and my plans into Your hands and receive what You want for me. Protect me from the influence of tempting shortcuts to the expected end You've promised. All the earth is Yours, Lord, and I receive my inheritance through Christ Jesus by the guidance of the Holy Spirit. You're my master orchestrator and the author and finisher of my faith. Thank You for who You are and all You do. You are worthy of all praise. In Jesus' name I pray. Amen.

###

About the Author

Chantale Williams was born in Montreal, Canada, to Haitian entrepreneurs who moved to the United States when she was about two years old. She grew up in Connecticut; there her parents kept close ties with the local Haitian community, which helped Chantale retain her native tongue.

At the age of sixteen, she and her family moved to Belize, where she graduated high school and learned basic Spanish. Chantale's fondest memories of those years include working at the Broadcasting Corporation of Belize selling radio commercial spots. Her employers soon discovered the marketability of her voice and asked her to voice commercial spots for their top clients, fill in as a disc jockey, deliver the daily news, and sing the Belizean national anthem at government functions.

Chantale later returned to the United States and joined the army as a finance specialist. Her first duty assignment was Fort Lewis, Washington (now Joint Base Lewis-McChord), where she met her husband,

Elton, also in the army. They were later reassigned to Ansbach, Germany; there Chantale ended her military career upon tour completion.

Elton and Chantale were then assigned to Fort Hood, Texas, where their two children, Vivianna and Elton Jr., were born. While at Fort Hood, Chantale pursued entrepreneurial endeavors and further education; she graduated magna cum laude with a bachelor of science in technical management with a concentration in accounting and holds a master of business administration. She is currently employed as an auditor.

Chantale is also a singer-songwriter, blogger, and entrepreneur, and a member of several professional organizations. In addition to her writing she enjoys traveling and has volunteered at local churches for many years, serving in the choir, children's ministry, women's ministry, business ministry, and other positions of leadership.

Elton and Chantale currently reside in Chantilly, Virginia. God is truly up to something big in their lives, and they continue to enjoy this adventure of faith.

Thank you for reading my book. If you enjoyed it, please take a moment to leave me a review at your favorite retailer.

Thanks!

Chantale Williams

Visit my website at:

http://www.chantalewilliams.com

www.ingramcontent.com/pod-product-compliance
Lightning Source LLC
LaVergne TN
LVHW021453080426
835509LV00018B/2263